AF316643

52 Weeks of Systematic Theology for Teens

A Complete Yearlong Guide to Understanding What Christians Believe, Why It's True, and How It Applies to Real Life

Welcome Aboard, Check Out This Limited-Time Free Bonus!

Ahoy, reader! Welcome to the Ahoy Publications family, and thanks for snagging a copy of this book! Since you've chosen to join us on this journey, we'd like to offer you something special.

Check out the link below for a FREE e-book filled with delightful facts about American History.

But that's not all - you'll also have access to our exclusive email list with even more free e-books and insider knowledge. Well, what are ye waiting for? Click the link below to join and set sail toward exciting adventures in American History.

Access your bonus here

https://ahoypublications.com/

Or, Scan the QR code!

Table of Contents

INTRODUCTION

You already believe things.

You believe your friends will show up. You believe your phone alarm will go off. You believe a teacher will grade your work. You believe you can trust some people, and you can't trust others.

Beliefs shape choices. Choices shape your life.

Systematic theology is just a big name for a simple idea: **putting what the Bible teaches into clear groups, so you can know what you believe, why it's true, and how to live it.**

This book is for teenagers who want faith that can stand up in real life. Not faith that works only at youth group. Not faith that falls apart the first time someone asks a hard question. Faith that holds when you're stressed, tempted, confused, or hurting.

We will talk about God. We will talk about you. We will talk about Jesus. We will talk about truth, sin, grace, and the future. And we will keep coming back to one place: **God's Word.**

What this book will help you do

By the end of these 52 weeks, you will be able to:

- **Explain the gospel clearly** without getting lost or going blank.
- **Read the Bible with more confidence**, not just random verses.
- **Spot fake "Christian" ideas** that sound kind but deny God's truth.
- **Handle doubt in a healthy way**, without hiding it or feeding it.
- **Make wiser choices** with your body, words, time, and friends.
- **Understand why Jesus matters every day**, not just on Easter.

You will also build something most people don't build on purpose: a strong "belief map." When life hits, you won't be trying to invent answers on the spot. You'll already know what God says, and you'll know where to go in Scripture.

What theology is (in plain words)

Theology means "words about God."

Systematic theology means "sorting Bible truth into topics."

So instead of saying, "I think God is like this," you learn to say, "Scripture teaches this, and here's why."

That matters because opinions change fast. Feelings change fast too. God does not.

Why teens should care

Because you are already getting trained by something.

Every day, messages aim at you:

- "You are what you feel."
- "Truth is whatever works for you."
- "Your body is yours, so do what you want."
- "If God is loving, He would never say no."
- "People are basically good, and sin is just a mistake."

Some of those lines sound kind. Some sound strong. Many sound free.

But here's the problem: **a lie can feel freeing at first, then trap you later.**

God's truth can feel hard at first, then bring peace later.

This book won't treat you like you're stupid. It also won't pretend you're your own savior. It will take you seriously, and it will take the Bible seriously.

What this book is (and isn't)

This book is:

- **Bible-centered**: we start with Scripture, not trending opinions.
- **Clear and practical**: truth you can use on Monday, not just Sunday.
- **Honest**: we talk about doubt, sin, shame, suffering, and pressure.

This book is not:

- A "try harder" book.
- A list of religious rules to impress adults.
- A set of shallow answers to deep questions.

Christian faith is not about cleaning yourself up so God will like you. It's about God saving you in Jesus, then changing you from the inside out.

How the 52 weeks work

Each week is one lesson. You can do it in about 15-20 minutes.

Here's a simple plan:

1. **Read the main idea** and the Bible passages.
2. **Write a one-sentence summary** in your own words.
3. **Answer the questions** honestly (no need to sound "spiritual").
4. **Do the action step** for the week.
5. **Pray one short prayer** based on what you learned.

If you miss a week, don't quit. Just keep going. Growth is not about being perfect. It's about staying close to Jesus.

A quick warning (in a helpful way)

Systematic theology can be used in a bad way.

Some people learn Bible facts to win arguments. Others use theology to feel better than people who don't know as much.

That's not the goal here.

If your theology does not lead to love, humility, and obedience, something is off. Truth is meant to shape your life, not just fill your head.

The goal is not to be "the smart Christian." The goal is to be a faithful Christian.

Your "belief map" (why this matters)

Think of faith like a map for a long trip.

If your map is wrong, it doesn't matter how confident you feel. You still get lost.

Systematic theology helps you build a map that matches reality because it comes from God's Word.

Here are the big topics you'll cover:

- **God's Word**: why it's trustworthy and how to read it well
- **God**: His character and the Trinity
- **People**: the image of God, sin, and our need
- **Jesus**: who He is and what He did
- **The Holy Spirit**: how God changes you
- **Salvation**: grace, faith, repentance, growth, and suffering
- **The Church**: community, leadership, gifts, and conflict
- **Christian living**: prayer, wisdom, purity, honesty, work, money, justice, and sharing faith
- **Standing firm**: answering big questions and spotting false teaching
- **What's next**: resurrection, judgment, and new creation hope

That's the full year. One week at a time.

If you feel unsure, you're not alone

Maybe you grew up in church but still feel confused.

Maybe you believe in Jesus, but you don't know how to explain why.

Maybe you've messed up in ways you don't talk about.

Maybe you're tired of fake answers.

Here's what I want you to know from the start:

- God can handle your honest questions.
- Jesus is not scared of your weakness.
- Grace is real, and it changes people.
- Truth is good, even when it corrects you.

You don't have to clean up first. Come to Christ. Then He will clean you.

One simple prayer to begin

God, please teach me what is true. Help me love You with my mind and my life. Help me trust Jesus. Help me obey You when it's hard. Change me from the inside. Amen.

PART ONE
Trust God's Word

WEEK 1
Open the Bible with Confidence
What the Bible Is

Some books give advice. Some books tell stories. Some books teach facts.

The Bible is different.

The Bible is **God's Word written down.** That means when you open it, you are not just reading old thoughts from smart people. You are hearing God speak through human authors.

That should change how you read it.

It also should calm you down. You do not have to guess what God is like. You do not have to invent your purpose. God has spoken.

The big idea

The Bible is God's true Word, given through human writers, so you can know God, trust His promises, and live wisely.

Key Bible passages (read these first)

- **2 Timothy 3:16–17** - Scripture comes from God and trains you for life.
- **2 Peter 1:20–21** - God used human writers, and the Spirit guided them.
- **Psalm 19:7–11** - God's Word is good, clear, and worth more than gold.
- **Hebrews 4:12** - God's Word is living and exposes what's in you.

What the Bible is

The Bible is a library, not one single book. It has **66 books:**

- **39** in the Old Testament
- **27** in the New Testament

It was written across many centuries by many human authors. There are different types of writing, like:

- history
- poetry
- letters
- prophecy
- wisdom writing

Even with all that variety, the Bible tells one main story: **God saves sinners through Jesus Christ.**

The Old Testament points forward to Him. The New Testament shows His life, death, resurrection, and the growth of His church.

How God gave us the Bible

Here's the simple, Bible-based answer:

- God chose human writers.
- They wrote in their own style and words.
- God's Spirit guided them so their words were also God's words.

That's what people mean when they say the Bible is "inspired." The idea is not, "The writers felt creative." The idea is, **God breathed out Scripture** (2 Timothy 3:16).

So the Bible is both:

- **fully human** (real writers, real history, real language), and
- **fully God's Word** (true, trustworthy, and carrying His authority)

If you've ever wondered, "Is it okay to question the Bible?" here's a better question:

Will I let the Bible question me?

Because it will.

What the Bible is for

A lot of teens treat the Bible like it has one job: make you feel better.

Sometimes it does comfort you. But that is not its only job.

According to 2 Timothy 3:16–17, Scripture is useful for:

- **teaching** (showing what is true)
- **reproof** (showing what is wrong)
- **correction** (showing how to get back on track)
- **training in righteousness** (showing how to live wisely)

So the Bible helps you in two big ways:

1. **It shows you God.**

2. **It shapes you to live God's way.**

That means the Bible is not mainly a self-help book.

It's a God-revealing book.

One key truth teens need to hear

If you only read the Bible to find quick answers, you can miss the main point.

The Bible is not a set of random quotes. It is a message.

And the center of the message is Jesus.

Jesus said the Scriptures point to Him (John 5:39). After His resurrection, He showed His disciples how the Old Testament was about Him (Luke 24:27).

So when you read the Bible, keep asking:

✝ What does this show me about God?

✝ What does this show me about people?

✝ How does this connect to Jesus?

✝ What should change in me because of this?

Common confusion

"The Bible was written by people, so it must be full of mistakes."

People do make mistakes.

But the claim of the Bible is that God guided the writers, so what they wrote is true. God is not careless. God does not lie (Titus 1:2).

That does not mean every verse is easy. It does not mean you will never have questions. It means you have a strong place to stand when you do.

"Is the Bible just one religion's opinion?"

Christianity is not built on "I feel like God is real."

It is built on God speaking and acting in history, especially through Jesus. The Bible gives eyewitness-based writing in the New Testament and centuries of God's promises in the Old Testament.

You'll learn more about why the Bible is true in Week 3. This week, we start with what it is: **God speaking to His people.**

Real life: how this helps you this week

When you're stressed, it's easy to follow your feelings.

When you're tempted, it's easy to follow your friends.

When you're hurt, it's easy to follow anger.

But if the Bible is God's Word, then you have something steadier than all of that.

This week, you're not trying to become a Bible expert.

You are doing one simple thing: **opening the Bible like it matters.**

Quick check (answer in your own words)

1. What does it mean that the Bible is "God's Word"?

2. Why does it matter that God used human writers?

3. What is one reason you personally want to read the Bible this year? Be honest.

4. Which is harder for you: believing the Bible is true, or living like it's true? Why?

Memory

> *"All Scripture is God-breathed and is useful for teaching,*
> *rebuking, correcting and training in righteousness," -*
> *2 Timothy 3:16*

Action step for the week

Pick one Gospel (Matthew, Mark, Luke, or John). Choose the one that feels easiest to start.

Then do this for **5 days**:

1. Read **one chapter.**

2. Write **one sentence**: "This shows me that Jesus is..."

____

____

____

3. Pray one short prayer: "Jesus, help me trust You today."

That's it. Keep it simple. Keep it steady.

Closing prayer

God, thank You for speaking. Help me listen. Help me read Your Word with respect and joy. Help me trust what You say, even when my feelings are loud. Please change me through Your truth. Amen.

WEEK 2
Know What Counts
How We Got the Bible
(Canon Basics)

Have you ever heard someone say, "The Bible is just a bunch of books people picked"?

Or, "Some leaders edited it to control people"?

Those lines sound confident. They also sound like a mystery movie.

This week clears the fog.

Christians did not sit in a room and *make* the Bible God's Word. God's Word was God's Word from the moment it was written. The big question was simpler:

Which writings did God give to His people?

That collection is called the **canon.**

The big idea

The canon is the set of books God gave to His people, and the church recognized them because they carried God's authority.

Key Bible passages (read these first)

- **Luke 24:44** - Jesus speaks of the Law, Prophets, and Psalms (a common way to describe the Old Testament).

- **1 Thessalonians 2:13** - God's Word is received as God's Word, not as human words.

- **2 Peter 3:15–16** - Peter treats Paul's letters like "Scriptures."

- **Revelation 22:18–19** - a warning about adding to or taking away from God's words (in its context, it refers to Revelation, but it shows God cares about guarding His message).

What "canon" means

The word "canon" means a **rule** or **measuring stick**.

So "the canon of Scripture" means: **the official list of books that are Scripture.**

For most Christians, that list is:

✝ **39 books** in the Old Testament

✝ **27 books** in the New Testament

Total: **66 books**

A helpful picture

Think of it like this:

✝ God gives the books.

✝ God's people recognize the books.

✝ The church does not create Scripture. The church receives it.

So the canon is not about humans giving the Bible authority. It is about humans **submitting** to the authority God already gave.

How the Old Testament books were recognized

In Jesus' day, the Jewish people already had recognized sacred writings. Jesus referred to them as a complete group.

In Luke 24:44, He points to the three-part set often described as:

✝ the Law (Genesis–Deuteronomy),

✝ the Prophets,

✝ the Psalms (a way of speaking about the Writings, which includes Psalms and other books).

That matters because Jesus treated those writings as God's Word. He quoted them. He obeyed them. He said they could not be broken (see John 10:35).

So Christians receive the Old Testament not because it is old, but because:

✝ Jesus affirmed it as Scripture, and

✝ it had already been recognized as God's Word among God's people.

How the New Testament books were recognized

The New Testament did not drop from the sky as one book.

It came through:

✝ **the apostles** (Jesus' chosen witnesses), and

✝ their close companions (like Mark and Luke).

The early church used clear tests to recognize which writings were truly from God. Here are four simple ones:

1. **Apostolic source**

   Was it written by an apostle, or by someone closely connected to an apostle?

2. **True teaching**

   Did it agree with what Jesus and the apostles taught everywhere?

3. **Wide use in churches**

   Was it read and used across many churches, not just one small group?

4. **Clear spiritual weight**

   Did it carry the marks of God's truth and power?

That does not mean the church "voted" books into Scripture like a talent show.

It means the church **recognized** what God had already given.

And we can see this recognition happening inside the Bible itself. One example is 2 Peter 3:15–16, where Peter refers to Paul's letters and links them with "the other Scriptures." That shows Christians were already treating apostolic writings as Scripture very early.

What about "lost books" and "extra gospels"?

You might hear about "other gospels" or "hidden books" that were "left out."

Here's the simple truth:

Some ancient writings claimed to be Christian but were not written by apostles. Many came much later and taught things that did not match Jesus and the apostles.

Some were interesting historically. Some were confusing. Some were plainly false.

The early church did not toss them out because leaders were scared.

They rejected them because they did not meet the tests:

✝ no real apostolic source,

✝ teaching that clashed with the gospel,

✝ not widely received as Scripture.

So if someone says, "They hid the real books," ask:

✝ Who wrote them?

✝ When were they written?

✝ Do they match the teaching Jesus gave?

✝ Were they accepted across the churches early on?

Questions like that cut through the drama fast.

A clear note about Bible translations

You may also wonder, "If the Bible is true, why are there so many translations?"

A translation is not a new Bible. It is the same message moved into a new language.

Some translations are more word-for-word. Others are more thought-for-thought. That can affect style, but it does not erase the message.

If you can, use a reliable translation and stick with it for this year. If your church recommends one, start there.

Real life: why this matters for you

If you think the Bible is just a human collection, you'll treat it like advice you can accept or ignore.

But if God gave these books, then Scripture has a claim on you.

That can feel heavy, but it is also freeing.

Because it means:

✝ truth is not invented,

✝ hope is not wishful thinking,

✝ and your faith is not built on rumors.

It is built on God speaking through real people in real history.

Quick check (answer in your own words)

1. What does "canon" mean?

____

____

____

____

2. Why is it important that the church recognized Scripture instead of creating it?

----

3. Name two simple tests the early church used to recognize New Testament books.

----

4. What is one claim you've heard about "lost books," and how would you respond after this lesson?

Memory verse

"And we also thank God continually because, when you received the word of God, which you heard from us, you accepted it not as a human word, but as it actually is, the word of God, which is indeed at work in you who believe." — 1 Thessalonians 2:13

Action step for the week

Do one short "Bible confidence" practice:

1. Write this sentence in your notes:

   "I don't stand over the Bible. I sit under it."

   ----

2. Then pick one New Testament letter (James, 1 Peter, or Ephesians are good starts).

3. Read just **one chapter** and answer two lines:
    o "This shows God is..." _______________________________
    o "This calls me to..." _______________________________

Keep it honest and simple.

Closing prayer

God, thank You for guarding Your Word. Help me trust what You have given. Help me listen with a willing heart. Please make Your truth clear to me, and help me obey it. Amen.

WEEK 3
Trust What God Said
Why the Bible Is True

Lots of people say, "That's your truth."

But the Bible does not speak that way.

The Bible speaks like this: **"Thus says the Lord."**

So the big question is simple: **Can you trust it?**

This week won't answer every question you could ever ask. But it will give you strong reasons to stand on, even when someone tries to shake you.

The big idea

You can trust the Bible because God tells the truth, Jesus trusted Scripture, and the Bible's message fits real history and real life.

Key Bible passages (read these first)

- ✝ **Psalm 119:160** - God's Word is true.
- ✝ **John 17:17** - Jesus says God's Word is truth.
- ✝ **Matthew 5:17–18** - Jesus treats Scripture as lasting and serious.
- ✝ **Titus 1:2** - God does not lie.
- ✝ **Luke 1:1–4** - Luke explains careful eyewitness work.

Reason 1: God tells the truth

This is the base layer.

If God lies, nothing is safe.

But Scripture says God is true and cannot lie (Titus 1:2). That means when God speaks, His words are reliable. His words don't "age out." They don't break when culture changes.

So when the Bible says, "God spoke," it is claiming something huge: **the God who cannot lie has spoken to you.**

Reason 2: Jesus trusted the Bible

If you follow Jesus, you can't treat the Bible like it's optional.

Jesus quoted Scripture when He faced temptation (Matthew 4). He corrected people by saying, "Have you not read?" He taught from the Old Testament and treated it as God's Word.

In John 17:17, Jesus prayed, "Your word is truth."

So here's a simple thought:

If you trust Jesus, and Jesus trusted Scripture, then you have strong reason to trust Scripture too.

Reason 3: The Bible is rooted in real history

The Bible is not written like a fairy tale that starts with, "Once upon a time."

Luke begins his Gospel by saying he looked into things carefully and wrote an orderly account so his reader could know the truth (Luke 1:1–4). The New Testament writers talk about rulers, places, dates, travel, and real events.

Christianity is not built on "I had a warm feeling."

It is built on God acting in history, especially in the life, death, and resurrection of Jesus.

Reason 4: The Bible reads you

This part can feel uncomfortable, but it's also a clue.

The Bible does not flatter you.

It calls out pride, envy, lust, greed, bitterness, and fear. It names what we often hide. Hebrews 4:12 says God's Word exposes what's going on inside.

A fake holy book usually tells you what you want to hear. Scripture often tells you what you need to hear.

Then it gives real hope: forgiveness, change, and new life in Christ.

What about hard questions?

You might wonder:

- "What about contradictions?"
- "What about science?"
- "What about suffering?"
- "What about people who misuse the Bible?"

Those are real questions.

This week's anchor is this: **A hard passage is not the same thing as a false book.**

Many questions have good answers when you read carefully, check context, and learn what the text actually says. Also, people can twist anything. Abuse of the Bible does not cancel the Bible.

Real life: how this helps you this week

- ☐ When you're tired, your feelings can lead you.
- ☐ When you're angry, your friends can lead you.
- ☐ When you're tempted, your body can lead you.

But God's Word gives you a steady voice that does not change with your mood.

So this week, your goal is simple: **Treat the Bible like truth, then act like it's truth.**

Quick check (answer in your own words)

1. What is one reason you think the Bible is trustworthy?

   ____

   ____

   ____

   ____

2. How does Jesus' view of Scripture shape your view?

   ____

   ____

   ____

   ____

3. What's one hard question you have about the Bible right now? Write it down.

   ____

   ____

   ____

   ____

4. What is one area where you obey feelings more than Scripture?

____

____

____

____

Memory verse

"Sanctify them by the truth; your word is truth." -
John 17:17

Action step for the week

Do a "truth test" for 5 days:

1. Read **Psalm 119:9–16** (it's short).
2. Write one line: **"God's Word is true, so today I will ______ ."**

____

____

____

3. Do that one thing before the day ends.

Small obedience builds real strength.

Closing prayer

God, thank You for telling the truth. Help me trust Your Word even when I feel unsure. Give me a willing heart. Help me obey You in small ways this week. Please grow my faith. Amen.

WEEK 4
Read It Right: How to Understand the Bible Without Twisting It

Have you ever opened the Bible, read a verse, and thought, "What does that even mean?"

You're not alone.

The Bible is clear in what you need most, but it is not always simple at first glance. It's made of many books, written in real places, to real people, with real problems. If you ignore that, you can make a verse say almost anything.

That's called twisting.

This week helps you read the Bible in a way that is fair, honest, and safe.

The big idea

Read the Bible by paying attention to context, the type of writing, and the main point, so you hear what God meant, not just what you want.

Key Bible passages (read these first)

- ✝ **Nehemiah 8:8** - God's people read Scripture and "gave the sense," so people understood.

- ✝ **2 Timothy 2:15** - handle God's Word rightly.

- ✝ **2 Peter 3:16** - some twist Scripture, and it harms them.

- ✝ **Luke 24:27** - Jesus shows how Scripture fits together and points to Him.

Step 1: Start with the context (don't grab a random line)

A verse has a home.

Ask three simple questions:

1. **What comes before and after this verse?**
2. **Who is speaking, and who is being spoken to?**
3. **What is the situation?**

Here's why it matters.

If your friend texts you, "Fine. Do whatever," you would not understand that text unless you knew the conversation before it.

Same with Scripture.

Rule: Don't build a belief on one line if you have not read the paragraph.

Step 2: Notice the type of writing

The Bible uses different kinds of writing. That changes how you read it.

- **History** (like Exodus, Acts): tells what happened
- **Poetry** (like Psalms): uses pictures and strong feelings
- **Wisdom** (like Proverbs): general truths for wise living
- **Letters** (like Ephesians): teaching for churches
- **Prophecy** (like Isaiah): God's message, often calling people back

Example:

Proverbs often gives a pattern, not a promise for every situation.

Psalm writers often speak with emotion, but they still speak truth.

So don't read poetry like a science textbook. Don't read a proverb like a legal contract.

Step 3: Look for the author's main point

Bible reading is not a scavenger hunt for a line that fits your mood.

Ask: **What is the main point here?**

Here's a quick way to find it:

- Read the paragraph once.
- Then write a title for it in 7 words or less.

If you can't write a short title, you might not have the point yet.

Step 4: Let Scripture explain Scripture

The Bible is not a pile of disconnected thoughts. It fits together.

So if a verse is confusing, do this:

- ☐ Read more around it.
- ☐ Look for other verses on the same topic.
- ☐ Choose the clear passages to help you with the harder ones.

This protects you from strange ideas.

Step 5: Keep Jesus in the center

The whole Bible is not a list of heroes you should copy.

Yes, there are examples to learn from. But the main message is bigger: God saves sinners through Jesus.

Jesus taught His disciples that the Scriptures point to Him (Luke 24:27).

So ask:

- ☐ How does this passage show God's character?
- ☐ How does it show what people are like?
- ☐ How does it point to Jesus or the need for Him?
- ☐ How should a follower of Jesus respond?

Two common ways people twist the Bible

Let's name two big ones.

Twist #1: Using a verse as a slogan

This is when someone takes one verse, removes it from context, and uses it like a poster.

Example: "I can do all things through him who strengthens me" (Philippians 4:13).

That verse is real and true. But in context, Paul is talking about contentment in hardship, not winning every game or getting every goal.

So a verse can be true, and still be misused.

Twist #2: Making the Bible say what it never said

This is when someone reads their own idea into the text.

A simple warning sign:

If your meaning would shock the original readers, you probably went off track.

A simple method you can use every time (the "3C" method)

Use this in any passage:

1. **Context** - What's happening? Who is speaking?
2. **Claim** - What is the main truth being taught?
3. **Change** - What should I believe, do, or pray because of this?

That's it. It works in Psalms, in the Gospels, and in letters.

Real life: how this helps you this week

Bad Bible reading can do damage.

It can:

✝ make God look mean when He is not,

✝ make you feel crushed by guilt with no hope,

✝ make you proud and harsh,

✝ or make you believe things God never said.

Good Bible reading builds a steady life.

It helps you:

✝ know what is true,

✝ spot lies faster,

✝ and walk with God through real pressure.

Quick check (answer in your own words)

1. Why is context important? Give one reason.

____

____

____

____

2. Name two types of Bible writing and how they differ.

____

____

____

____

3. What is one way people twist Scripture?

____

____

____

____

4. Use the 3C method on a short passage you read this week.

____

____

____

____

Memory verse

*"Do your best to present yourself to God as one approved,
a worker who does not need to be ashamed and who
correctly handles the word of truth." - 2 Timothy 2:15*

Action step for the week

Use the 3C method for 4 days in a row.

Pick one short passage each day:

- Mark 1:40–45
- Psalm 23
- Ephesians 2:8–10
- James 1:19–27

For each one, write:

- Context (1–2 lines)

____

____

____

- Claim (1 sentence)

____

____

- Change (1 action you will take today)

____

____

Keep it short. Keep it honest.

Closing prayer

God, please help me read Your Word the right way. Protect me from twisting it. Give me a teachable heart. Help me see Jesus clearly and obey what You say. Amen.

WEEK 5
Spot the Difference:
God's Word vs. Opinions Online

You scroll for five minutes and get a hundred messages.

Some are funny. Some are angry. Some sound wise. Some sound "spiritual." Some even use Bible verses.

But here's the hard truth: **not every confident voice is a true voice.**

The internet can spread helpful things fast. It can also spread lies fast. And many lies don't look like lies at first. They look like "common sense."

This week will help you test what you hear, so you don't get pulled around by every loud opinion.

The big idea

God's Word is the final authority, so you should test every message by Scripture, not by popularity or feelings.

Key Bible passages (read these first)

- **Acts 17:11** - the Bereans checked teaching against Scripture.
- **1 John 4:1** - test the spirits; not every message is from God.
- **Colossians 2:8** - don't get captured by empty ideas.
- **Psalm 1:1–3** - two paths: listening to the wrong voices or delighting in God's Word.

Why this matters so much

A lot of people treat truth like a voting contest.

If lots of people agree, it must be right.

But truth is not decided by likes, shares, or comments.

If God is real, and if He has spoken, then His Word has more weight than every trending clip put together.

That doesn't mean you stop thinking. It means you stop treating the loudest voice as the best voice.

The problem with "hot takes"

A hot take usually has three ingredients:

1. **Confidence**
2. **Speed**
3. **No patience for context**

That's the opposite of wisdom.

God's Word teaches you to slow down, listen, and think clearly.

Four tests you can use right away

When you hear a claim online, run these tests. You can do this in under a minute.

Test 1: Scripture test - "Where does the Bible say that?"

This is the most important one.

Ask:

✝ Is this clearly taught in Scripture?

✝ Or is someone using one verse as a weapon?

✝ Is the verse in context?

If someone can't show it from Scripture, treat it as an opinion, even if it sounds holy.

Test 2: Jesus test - "Does this sound like Jesus?"

This is not "Does it sound nice?"

It's:

✝ Does it fit what Jesus taught?

✝ Does it match His character?

✝ Does it lead people to trust Him and obey Him?

Some messages talk about "God" but avoid Jesus. That should make you careful.

Test 3: Fruit test - "What does this produce?"

Bad teaching often produces:

✝ pride

✝ fear

✝ cruelty

+ obsession

+ confusion

+ excuses for sin

Good teaching tends to produce:

+ humility

+ courage

+ repentance

+ love

+ clear thinking

+ steady obedience

This doesn't mean good teaching always feels good. Scripture can correct you. But correction from God leads to life, not chaos.

Test 4: Authority test - "Who is in charge here?"

Some online messages treat God like a side character.

The person speaking is the star. Their feelings are the rule. Their experience is the proof.

But in Christianity, **God is God,** and we submit to Him.

A warning sign is when someone says things like:

+ "God would never..."

+ "My truth is..."

+ "You don't need the Bible for that..."

If they push God's Word to the side, they are pushing God to the side.

Two common traps for teens

Let's name them, because naming traps helps you see them.

Trap 1: "If it feels true, it is true."

Feelings matter, but feelings are not a compass for truth.

You can feel peace and still be wrong. You can feel anxious and still be right. God's Word is steady when you are not.

Trap 2: "If it sounds loving, it must be right."

Love is not the same as letting people do whatever they want.

God's love is holy love. It tells the truth. It warns. It rescues.

Jesus was full of grace and truth (John 1:14). Keep both together.

A clear example (how verses get misused)

Sometimes people use this verse:

"Judge not, that you be not judged" (Matthew 7:1).

Some use it to shut down any talk about sin.

But keep reading. Jesus goes on to say:

- ✝ take the log out of your own eye first,
- ✝ then help your brother with the speck.

So Jesus is not saying, "Never judge anything."

He is saying, "Don't judge like a hypocrite."

That's why context matters.

Real life: what to do when you see a "Christian" clip online

Here's a simple plan.

1. **Pause.** Don't instantly share it.
2. **Ask:** What is the main claim? Write it in one sentence.
3. **Open your Bible:** Is that claim taught clearly in Scripture?
4. **Check the tone:** Does it push you toward Jesus and holiness?
5. **Ask a trusted adult:** a parent, pastor, or mature believer if you're unsure.

This is not about being suspicious of everyone.

It's about being careful with your mind and heart.

Quick check (answer in your own words)

1. Why is popularity not a good test for truth?

    ____

    ____

    ____

    ____

2. What is one of the four tests you need most right now? Why?

    ____

    ____

    ____

    ____

3. What is a warning sign that a message is pushing Scripture aside?

____

____

____

____

4. Think of a "Christian" message you've heard recently. How would you test it?

____

____

____

____

Memory verse

"Dear friends, do not believe every spirit, but test the spirits to see whether they are from God, because many false prophets have gone out into the world." —
1 John 4:1

Action step for the week

Do the "One-Post Test" three times this week.

Pick one post, clip, or quote that talks about faith.

Then write four short lines:

- **Claim:** What is it saying?
- **Scripture:** What verse supports or corrects it?
- **Fruit:** What attitude does it produce?
- **Next step:** Share, save, ignore, or ask someone?

This trains you to think before you agree.

Closing prayer

God, please guard my mind. Help me love truth more than being liked. Give me wisdom to test what I hear. Help me stay close to Jesus and to Your Word. Amen.

WEEK 6
Use Scripture Daily:
Build a Habit That Stays

Most people don't quit Bible reading because they hate God.

They quit because they get busy, tired, distracted, or bored.

They miss a day, then feel guilty, then avoid it, then weeks pass.

So this week is not about hype. It's about a plan you can keep.

A real habit is small enough to do on hard days.

The big idea

Daily Bible time is how you stay close to God, renew your mind, and grow steady faith.

Key Bible passages (read these first)

- **Psalm 1:1–3** - the steady person delights in God's Word.
- **Joshua 1:8** - keep God's Word close so you can live wisely.
- **Matthew 4:4** - you need God's Word like you need food.
- **James 1:22–25** - don't just hear the Word; do it.

What a Bible habit is (and what it isn't)

A Bible habit is not a way to earn God's love.

God's love is a gift in Christ.

A Bible habit is also not a way to prove you're "a good Christian."

A Bible habit is a way to keep hearing God's truth so your life does not get shaped by lies.

Think of it like this:

- If you only eat once a week, you get weak.
- If you only hear God's Word once a week, your faith can get weak too.

You can still be saved and struggle at the same time. But God calls you to grow.

Why habits beat moods

Some days you will feel like reading.

Many days you won't.

If you wait for the perfect mood, you'll read less than you want.

Habits help you stay faithful when you don't feel excited.

A good habit is like a small rail. It keeps your life from sliding off.

The "Small Plan That Stays"

Here is a plan that works even on busy school days.

It has three parts. It can take 7–12 minutes.

1) Read (3–6 minutes)

Read a short section. Don't try to read huge chunks at first.

A paragraph is fine. A chapter is fine. Keep it simple.

2) Write (2 minutes)

Write two lines:

- **God is...** (what the passage shows about God)

____

____

- **So I will...** (one response you can obey today)

____

____

That's it.

3) Pray (2–4 minutes)

Pray using your two lines.

Example:

"God, You are patient. Help me be patient with my sister today."

Pick a time and place (make it easy)

You don't need a perfect setup. You need a repeatable one.

Choose:

- **Time:** right after waking up, after school, or before bed
- **Place:** desk, couch, kitchen table, or outside
- **Tool:** Bible app or paper Bible (either is fine)

A tip that helps: Put your Bible where you already go every day.

If your phone is your alarm, put your Bible app on the first screen. If you eat breakfast, keep a Bible at the table.

Pick a reading path (no guessing)

Guessing what to read can kill a habit.

Here are three simple paths for teens:

Path A: Meet Jesus first

- Read **Mark** (fast and clear)
- Then read **John** (deep and personal)

Path B: Learn how Christians live

- Read **Ephesians**
- Then read **James**

Path C: Build prayer language

- Read **one Psalm each day**
- plus **one short New Testament passage**

Choose one path and stick with it for four weeks.

What to do when it feels boring

Sometimes the Bible will feel exciting.

Sometimes it will feel like homework.

When it feels boring, try one of these:

- Read out loud.
- Read a smaller chunk.
- Ask one question: "What does this show about God?"
- Write down one word that stands out, then look at the sentence around it.

____

____

Also, remember this: Boring often means you're reading too fast or too random.

Slow down. Stay in one book.

What to do when you miss a day

This part matters.

If you miss a day, do not punish yourself by quitting.

Do not say, "I failed."

Say: "I missed a day. I'm starting again today."

God's mercy is not fragile.

You can restart a thousand times. The goal is not perfection. The goal is closeness.

Real life: how Scripture changes your day

Scripture helps you in very normal teen moments:

- When friends pressure you, Scripture helps you stand firm.
- When you feel ugly or unwanted, Scripture reminds you of your worth in Christ.
- When you're angry, Scripture helps you slow down and speak wisely.
- When you're tempted, Scripture gives you truth to fight with.
- When you're anxious, Scripture calls you to trust God's care.

Psalm 1 says the person rooted in God's Word becomes like a tree planted by water.

Trees don't grow in one night.

They grow by steady feeding.

Quick check (answer in your own words)

1. Why is Bible reading not a way to earn God's love?

   ____

   ____

   ____

2. What time and place will you choose for your habit this week?

   ____

   ____

   ____

3. Which reading path will you choose (A, B, or C)?

   ____

   ____

   ____

4. What is your plan if you miss a day?

____

____

____

____

Memory verse

"Jesus answered, "It is written: 'Man shall not live on bread alone, but on every word that comes from the mouth of God.'" - Matthew 4:4

Action step for the week

Do the "Small Plan That Stays" for **6 days** this week.

Each day, write your two lines:

✝ **God is**

____

____

✝ **So I will**

____

____

At the end of the week, look back and circle **one repeated theme** you see about God (like His patience, holiness, kindness, or wisdom).

Closing prayer

God, please help me stay close to You. Give me a steady habit with Your Word. Help me listen, believe, and obey. When I mess up, help me start again. Thank You for Your patience with me. Amen.

PART TWO
Know the Living God

WEEK 7
Meet God as He Is:
God's Names and What They Show

Names matter.

A nickname can tell you how people see you. A title can tell you what role you have. A last name can connect you to a family story.

In the Bible, God's names are not random labels. They reveal who He is. They show His character. They help you know Him as He really is, not as you wish He would be.

This matters because it's easy to build a "god" in your mind that matches your mood. A god who never corrects you. A god who always agrees. A god who mainly wants you to feel fine.

But the real God is better than that.

The big idea

God's names reveal God's character, so you can trust Him, worship Him, and stop guessing what He is like.

Key Bible passages (read these first)

✝ **Exodus 3:13–15** - God tells Moses His name.

✝ **Exodus 34:5–7** - God describes His own character.

✝ **Psalm 9:10** - knowing God's name connects to trusting Him.

✝ **John 17:6** - Jesus makes the Father known.

Why God's names are a gift

You learn what someone is like by what they say and do.

But God is not like a classmate you can observe from far away. You need Him to reveal Himself.

And He does.

When God gives His name, He is saying, "This is who I am. You can count on Me."

That's why God's names show up in moments when people are scared, stuck, guilty, or unsure.

Name 1: "I AM" (YHWH) - God is self-existent and unchanging

In Exodus 3, Moses asks God what he should say when the people ask, "What is His name?"

God answers with a name that sounds strange at first:

"I AM WHO I AM."

Then He connects it to the name He wants Israel to use: **the LORD** (often printed in Bibles as LORD in all caps).

This name teaches at least two big truths:

1. **God depends on no one.**

   Everything else needs something: food, sleep, air, help, time. God does not. He simply is.

2. **God does not change.**

   People can be one way today and another way next month. God stays faithful to who He is.

Real life: When people let you down, God's name reminds you He is steady.

Name 2: "God" (Elohim) - God is powerful and above all

In Genesis 1, "God" creates. He speaks, and things exist.

This name points to God's strength and greatness.

Real life: When life feels big and you feel small, this name tells you you're not alone in a random universe. You live in God's world.

Name 3: "Lord" (Adonai) - God is the rightful ruler

"Lord" is a ruler word. It means master, owner, king.

If God is Lord, then He has the right to lead you.

This name pushes against one of the strongest teen lies: "Your life is your own."

Real life: When you don't want to obey, remember who God is. He's not your helper on the side. He's your King.

Name 4: Father - God is personal and caring

In the Bible, God is not only powerful. He is also personal.

Jesus teaches His followers to pray, "Our Father" (Matthew 6:9).

That doesn't mean God is soft or passive. It means He is loving, present, and committed.

A good father provides, protects, teaches, and corrects.

Real life: When you feel alone, God being Father means you can come close, not hide.

Name 5: "God Almighty" (El Shaddai) - God can keep His promises

God uses "Almighty" when He makes big promises to Abraham (see Genesis 17:1).

When God promises, He is not hoping it works out. He has power to do what He says.

Real life: When you wonder, "Can God really help me change?" this name says, "Yes."

God's "name list" is not the point

You do not need to memorize every Hebrew word to know God.

The point is simpler: **God reveals Himself so you can trust Him.**

Psalm 9:10 says those who know God's name put their trust in Him. That means knowing God is not just for your mind. It's for your fear, stress, and choices.

The most important place God shows His name

If you want to know what God is like, look at Jesus.

Jesus did not come to give you random tips. He came to show you the Father.

In John 17:6, Jesus says He has made the Father's name known.

That means:

✟ Jesus shows God's holiness and compassion.

✟ Jesus shows God's truth and patience.

✟ Jesus shows God's power and gentleness.

✟ Jesus shows God's hatred of sin and love for sinners.

If your picture of God doesn't fit Jesus, your picture is off.

Common mistake: using God's name like a lucky charm

Some people treat God's name like a magic word.

They say the right phrase, expect God to do what they want, then get mad when life stays hard.

But God's names are not tricks to control Him.

They are windows to know Him.

Real life: three ways to use God's names this week

1. **When you're anxious:**

    Pray, "LORD, You are steady. Help me trust You today."

2. **When you're tempted:**

    Say, "Lord, You rule me. Help me obey You right now."

3. **When you feel unseen:**

    Pray, "Father, You see me. Help me rest in Your care."

Short prayers can be real prayers.

Quick check (answer in your own words)

1. Why does God reveal His names in Scripture?

    ____

    ____

    ____

    ____

2. What does "I AM" teach you about God?

    ____

    ____

    ____

    ____

3. Which name or title of God do you struggle to believe in your daily life: Lord or Father? Why?

    ____

    ____

    ____

    ____

4. How does Jesus help you know what God is like?

    ____

    ____

    ____

    ____

Memory verse

"Those who know your name trust in you, for you, Lord, have never forsaken those who seek you." - Psalm 9:10

Action step for the week

Choose **one name/title** of God to focus on for 7 days:

LORD, Father, or **Lord.**

Each day, do this in 3 minutes:

1. Write the name at the top of your page.

2. Write one truth about God from today's reading.

3. Pray one sentence that starts with that name.

Example: "Father, thank You for staying near. Help me trust You at school today."

Closing prayer

God, thank You for showing me who You are. Please keep me from making You into what I want. Help me know You as You truly are. Help me trust You and worship You with my whole life. Amen.

WEEK 8
Hold on to God's Greatness: God Is Holy

"Holy" is one of those church words people hear a lot but don't always get.

Some teens think "holy" means "boring" or "perfect and far away."

The Bible means something better.

God's holiness is His clean, blazing goodness. He is not like us. He is pure. He is right. He is set apart from all sin. And He is worthy of your full respect.

If you miss this, you'll shrink God down. You'll treat Him like a helpful buddy. You'll shrug at sin. You'll wonder why worship feels small.

When you see God as holy, everything starts to make sense.

The big idea

God is holy, so you should treat Him with awe, hate sin, and run to Jesus for cleansing and courage.

Key Bible passages (read these first)

- **Isaiah 6:1–7** - Isaiah sees God's holiness and his own sin.
- **1 Peter 1:15–16** - God calls His people to be holy.
- **Revelation 4:8–11** - heaven worships God as holy.
- **Habakkuk 1:13** - God is pure and hates evil.

What "holy" means

In the Bible, "holy" means **set apart**.

God is set apart in two ways:

1. **He is morally pure.**

   No sin. No darkness. No hidden wrong.

2. **He is greater than everything He made.**

God is not part of creation. He rules creation.

So holiness is not just one trait among many. It's like the bright light that shines through all His traits.

- ✝ His love is holy love.
- ✝ His anger is holy anger.
- ✝ His justice is holy justice.
- ✝ His mercy is holy mercy.

Isaiah's moment: what happens when someone meets the holy God

Isaiah 6 shows this clearly.

Isaiah sees the Lord high and lifted up. Seraphim cry out:

"Holy, holy, holy is the LORD of hosts."

Then Isaiah doesn't say, "This is cool."

He says, **"Woe is me!"**

Why?

Because when you see God's holiness, you see your sin more clearly.

Isaiah admits, "I am a man of unclean lips, and I live among a people of unclean lips."

That's not just about bad words. Lips represent what comes out of your heart—lies, pride, harsh jokes, bragging, gossip, cruel comments, and dirty talk.

Isaiah's response is what honesty looks like.

Then something else happens: God cleanses him. A coal touches his lips, and he is forgiven.

Here's the pattern:

1. **God's holiness is revealed.**
2. **Sin is exposed.**
3. **God provides cleansing.**
4. **God sends the cleansed person to serve.**

That is still how God works.

Why God's holiness is good news

At first, holiness can feel scary.

Because if God is holy, then sin is serious.

But holiness is also good news because it means:

- God is never shady.
- God is never cruel.
- God is never dirty-minded.
- God is never unfair.
- God is never tempted.

You can trust Him fully because He is clean and right.

What holiness does to your view of sin

Sin is not just "messing up."

Sin is rebellion against a holy God.

That's why "small sins" are not small.

- A "small lie" attacks truth.
- "Small porn" trains your mind to use people.
- "Small gossip" tears down someone God made.
- "Small hate" poisons your heart.

If God is holy, then sin is not a joke.

But here's the hope:

God does not show you sin to crush you. He shows you sin so you will run to the Savior.

Holiness and Jesus (this is the center)

You might feel stuck here.

"If God is holy, how can I come close?"

The answer is Jesus.

Jesus is the Holy One who came near to unholy people without becoming unholy.

He touched lepers. He ate with sinners. He welcomed the ashamed. He forgave the guilty.

Then He took sin on Himself at the cross.

So you don't come to God by pretending you're clean.

You come to God by trusting Christ, who makes you clean.

"Be holy" doesn't mean "be fake"

1 Peter 1:15–16 says, "Be holy, for I am holy."

That does not mean:

+ act perfect,
+ hide your struggles,
+ pretend you never sin.

It means:

+ belong to God,
+ fight sin,
+ tell the truth,
+ keep turning back to Him.

Holiness looks like real repentance, not a perfect image.

Real life: how to live like God is holy

Here are three teen-level ways this hits your life this week.

1) Your words

Isaiah confessed "unclean lips."

Ask:

+ Do my words build up or tear down?
+ Do I say "sorry" when I sin with my mouth?
+ Do I joke about sin like it's harmless?

A holy God calls you to clean speech and honest apology.

2) Your private life

God sees what no one else sees.

Holiness means you don't live two lives:

+ one for people,
+ one in secret.

You will never grow strong by hiding.

3) Your worship

If God is holy, worship is not a performance.

It's a response.

Even when your voice cracks. Even when you're tired. Even when you don't feel it yet.

Quick check (answer in your own words)

1. What does "holy" mean in the Bible?

____

____

____

____

2. What happened to Isaiah when he saw God's holiness?

____

____

____

____

3. Why is God's holiness good news, not just scary news?

____

____

____

____

4. What is one area of your life where you need to treat sin as serious?

____

____

____

Memory verse

"Holy, holy, holy is the LORD of hosts." — Isaiah 6:3

Action step for the week

Do the "Isaiah 6 check" for 5 days:

1. Read **Isaiah 6:1–7** (or just verses 3–7 if you're short on time).
2. Write one line: **"God, You are holy, so I will _________ today."**
3. Pick one action that matches holiness:
   - apologize for harsh words,
   - delete something that feeds sin,
   - set a boundary for your phone,
   - tell the truth even if it costs you,
   - ask for help from a trusted adult.

Choose one small step and do it the same day.

Closing prayer

Holy God, I praise You for Your clean goodness. Please show me where I treat sin lightly. Forgive me through Jesus. Help me love what You love and hate what You hate. Make me more like Christ. Amen.

WEEK 9
Rest in God's Control: God Is Sovereign

There are days when life feels like a runaway shopping cart.

You didn't choose your family. You didn't choose your genetics. You didn't choose many of your problems. You can't control what other people do. You can't control the future.

And that can make you feel either panicky or numb.

The Bible gives a better option: **rest.**

Not because life is easy. But because God is sovereign.

"Sovereign" means God rules. He is King over everything. Nothing surprises Him. Nothing defeats Him. Nothing slips past Him.

The big idea

God is sovereign, so you can trust Him in chaos, pray with hope, and obey even when you don't know the outcome.

Key Bible passages (read these first)

- **Psalm 115:3** - God does what He pleases.
- **Daniel 4:34–35** - no one can stop God's hand.
- **Romans 8:28** - God works for good for those who love Him.
- **Proverbs 16:9** - you plan, but God directs your steps.

What "sovereign" does and doesn't mean

God's sovereignty means:

- God rules over creation.
- God rules over history.
- God rules over rulers.
- God rules over your life.

It does **not** mean:
- you are a robot,
- your choices don't matter,
- sin doesn't matter,
- pain doesn't matter.

The Bible teaches both truths at the same time:
- God is in control.
- humans make real choices and are responsible.

If you try to pick only one, you'll get weird fast.

A story that helps: Daniel 4

King Nebuchadnezzar was powerful. He thought he was untouchable.

God humbled him.

After it happened, the king said something huge:

God's rule is forever, and **no one can stop Him** (Daniel 4:34–35).

This is the point: even the strongest human leaders are not the final boss.

God is.

That matters when the news is scary or when your country feels unstable or when adults seem confused.

Where God's sovereignty shows up in your daily life

Sovereignty is not just a "big theology" idea. It hits normal teen life.

1) When you feel left out

You can start thinking, "God forgot me."

Sovereignty says: God sees you. Your life is not random. God can open doors no person can open.

2) When your family is messy

You might think, "This is ruining me."

Sovereignty says: God can meet you here, grow you here, and guide you through it. Your story is not over.

3) When you're scared of the future

You might think, "What if I fail?"

Sovereignty says: you can work hard without being crushed by fear. God is not guessing.

"God works for good" does not mean "life will feel good"

Romans 8:28 is one of the most quoted verses. It is also often misunderstood.

It does not say: "Everything that happens is good."

It says: God works **in** everything for good for those who love Him.

Sometimes God's good plan includes hard days. Sometimes His good is shaping your faith, rescuing you from sin, or building courage you'll need later.

God's good is bigger than comfort.

The best place to see sovereignty: the cross

If you ever wonder, "Is God really in control?" look at Jesus.

Jesus was not a victim of bad luck.

The cross was evil, and people were responsible. And at the same time, God used it to save sinners.

That means God can take the worst thing and bring the best rescue.

So when life feels out of control, Christianity does not give you a fake smile.

It gives you a strong anchor: **God rules, and He is wise and good.**

How sovereignty changes your prayer

Some teens don't pray because they think: "God already knows, so why bother?"

But the Bible teaches that God is sovereign **and** He tells you to pray.

Prayer is not you forcing God to do your plan.

Prayer is you coming to your Father and saying: "God, I trust You. Please help. Please lead. Please provide."

God often uses prayer as one of His chosen ways to act.

So sovereignty does not kill prayer.

It fuels it.

How sovereignty changes your choices

Here's where it gets practical.

If God is sovereign, you can obey even when you're not sure what will happen next.

You can:
- ✝ tell the truth even if it costs you,
- ✝ say no to sin even if friends laugh,
- ✝ forgive even if the other person stays rude,
- ✝ work hard even if you're not praised.

Because your life is not controlled by people's reactions.

God is in charge.

Quick check (answer in your own words)

1. What does it mean that God is sovereign?

____

____

____

____

2. What is one wrong idea people have about sovereignty?

____

____

____

____

3. How does God's sovereignty change the way you handle anxiety?

____

____

____

____

4. What is one area where you need to obey God and trust Him with the outcome?

____

____

____

____

Memory verse

*"Our God is in the heavens; he does all that he pleases." -
Psalm 115:3*

Action step for the week

Do the "Circle of Control" exercise once, then pray it daily.

1. Draw two circles (one inside the other).

2. In the inner circle write: **What I can control**
    - my words
    - my choices
    - my habits
    - my repentance

3. In the outer circle write: **What I can't control**
    - other people's actions
    - the future
    - opinions
    - outcomes

Then pray this each day: "God, help me obey You in what I can control, and trust You with what I can't."

Closing prayer

God, You rule over everything. Please help me stop acting like I have to carry the whole world. Give me peace. Help me make wise choices today. When I don't know what's next, help me trust You. Amen.

WEEK 10
Trust God's Heart:
God Is Good and Loving

A lot of people believe God is powerful.

But when life hurts, the harder question shows up:

Is God good?

If God is good, why does He allow pain? If God is loving, why does He say no to things I want? If God is kind, why does He correct me?

This week is about God's heart. Not the version people post online. The real God from Scripture.

God is good. God is loving. And He proves it most clearly in Jesus.

The big idea

God is good and loving, so you can trust Him, obey Him, and run to Him when you're hurting.

Key Bible passages (read these first)

- **Psalm 34:8** - taste and see that the LORD is good.
- **Psalm 136:1** - God is good; His love lasts forever.
- **Romans 5:8** - God shows His love in Christ's death for sinners.
- **1 John 4:9–10** - God's love is shown by sending His Son.

What "God is good" means

God's goodness is not just that He does nice things sometimes.

God is good in His nature.

That means:

- He always does what is right.
- He always does what is wise.
- He never does evil.
- He never acts out of selfishness.

Even when you don't understand His ways, His character stays clean.

What "God is loving" means

God's love is not a mood.

It is not God saying, "You can do anything you want and I'll clap."

God's love is committed care.

It means God:

- chooses to do good to His people,
- keeps His promises,
- corrects what destroys,
- and stays faithful even when you are not.

Real love protects. Real love tells the truth. Real love does not help you sin.

The biggest proof: Jesus

If you ever wonder what God's love looks like, don't start with your feelings. Start with the cross.

Romans 5:8 says God showed His love when Christ died for us **while we were still sinners**.

That means God didn't wait until you were cleaned up.

He moved toward you when you were guilty.

1 John 4 says love is not mainly about your love for God. It's about God's love for you, shown by sending His Son.

So God's love is not just words.

It's action.

"If God loves me, why is life hard?"

This is one of the most honest questions a teen can ask.

The Bible does not answer it by pretending pain is fake.

The Bible shows that:

- sin broke the world,
- people do evil,
- bodies get sick,
- relationships crack,
- and life can be unfair.

But it also shows that God can use hard things without being the author of evil.

A good parent sometimes allows hard things:

- training for sport is hard,
- studying for exams is hard,
- healing after injury can be hard.

Hard does not always mean harmful.

Sometimes God's love is seen in comfort. Sometimes it's seen in strength to endure. Sometimes it's seen in stopping you from becoming someone sin would ruin.

This doesn't make pain "nice." It makes pain not useless.

"If God is good, why does He say no?"

Because He sees what you can't.

A toddler might cry because they want to play in the street. A good parent says no.

God's "no" can feel painful. But it can also be protection.

God's commands are not random. They are gifts.

When God says no to sin, He is not stealing your joy. He is guarding it.

How God's goodness changes how you read the Bible

Some teens read commands and think, "God is trying to control me."

But if God is good and loving, then His commands are wise.

That changes your mindset from: "God is against me," to: "God is for me, so I can trust Him."

Psalm 34:8 says, "Taste and see that the LORD is good."

That's an invitation to experience God's goodness personally, not just talk about it.

Real life: where this hits you right now

Here are three areas where teens often struggle to trust God's heart.

1) When you mess up

You might think God is disgusted with you.

But the gospel says God welcomes repentant sinners through Jesus.

God's love is not fragile. Repentance is not you begging God to be kind. It's you returning to the One who already proved His love.

2) When you compare yourself

You might think, "God is good to them, but not to me."

Comparison lies.

God's goodness is not measured by who has the easiest life. It's measured by who has God.

If you have Christ, you have the biggest gift.

3) When you feel anxious

Anxiety whispers, "Something bad will happen, and you'll be alone."

God's goodness says, "You will not be alone."

That doesn't mean nothing hard will happen. It means God will not abandon you.

Quick check (answer in your own words)

1. What does it mean that God is good in His nature?

2. How is God's love different from a mood?

3. What does the cross show you about God's love?

4. Where do you struggle most to trust God's heart: pain, temptation, or the future?

Memory verse

"But God demonstrates his own love for us in this: While we were still sinners, Christ died for us." - Romans 5:8

Action step for the week

Do the "Goodness Journal" for 6 days.

Each day, write three short lines:

1. **God is good because...** (use a verse or truth from today's reading)

2. **I will trust Him by...** (one act of obedience)

3. **I will pray about...** (one real worry)

Suggested reading for the week:

- Day 1: Psalm 34
- Day 2: Psalm 136 (read a section)
- Day 3: Romans 5:1–11
- Day 4: 1 John 4:7–21
- Day 5: Matthew 11:28–30
- Day 6: Lamentations 3:19–26

Closing prayer

Good Father, thank You for Your love. Thank You for Jesus. Help me trust Your heart when life feels confusing. Help me obey You because You are good. Please comfort me in my pain and make me steady in faith. Amen.

WEEK 11
Tell the Truth About God: God Is Just

When you see unfairness, something in you reacts.

A teacher blames the wrong student. A friend gets bullied and no one helps. A cheater wins. Someone hurts your family and gets away with it.

That anger you feel is not always sin. Sometimes it's a clue.

You were made in God's image, and God is just.

God does what is right. He judges evil. He defends the weak. He never twists the rules. He never takes bribes. He never "plays favorites" the way people do.

And here's the part many miss: **God's justice is also the reason we need Jesus.**

The big idea

God is just, so evil matters, sin must be judged, and the cross becomes the clearest place where justice and mercy meet.

Key Bible passages (read these first)

- **Deuteronomy 32:4** - God is just and does no wrong.
- **Psalm 89:14** - justice is part of God's rule.
- **Romans 3:23–26** - God remains just while forgiving sinners through Jesus.
- **Micah 6:8** - God calls His people to do justice and love mercy.

What "God is just" means

God's justice means:

- God always does what is right.
- God always judges fairly.
- God treats sin as real, not as a joke.

✝ God protects what is good.

✝ God will make things right in the end.

God's justice is not like a moody person who snaps.

It is clean and right.

Deuteronomy 32:4 says God is faithful and just, and there is no wrong in Him.

That means:

✝ God never makes a bad call.

✝ God never overlooks evil because it's convenient.

✝ God never blames the wrong person.

Why this is hard for some teens

Some teens don't struggle to believe God is loving.

They struggle to believe God is just.

Because they see injustice everywhere.

And they think: "If God is just, why doesn't He stop this?"

That question matters, and Christians should not mock it.

The Bible's answer is not, "Stop asking."

The Bible shows three truths at the same time:

1. **Evil is real.**

2. **God is patient right now.**

3. **God will judge perfectly later.**

God's timing is not your timing. But His justice is not asleep.

God's patience is not God's weakness

When a person does wrong and doesn't get caught, it can look like God doesn't care.

But God's patience often gives time for repentance.

That does not erase justice. It delays it.

And the Bible is clear: delayed does not mean denied.

The cross: where justice and mercy meet

Here is the heart of Christianity:

God does not ignore sin. God does not pretend evil is fine.

So how can God forgive sinners and still be just?

Romans 3 answers it.

All have sinned. No one earns God's approval.

But God sent Jesus. Jesus took the punishment sin deserves. God judged sin at the cross.

So God can forgive those who trust Jesus and still be just, because sin was paid for.

This is why the cross is not only about love. It is also about justice.

If God waved sin away with no cost, He would not be just.

But God did not do that.

He paid the cost Himself in Christ.

Justice changes the way you see your sin

It's easy to think, "I'm not that bad."

But God's justice says sin is serious because God is holy and good.

That doesn't mean you live in shame.

It means you stop making excuses.

You confess. You turn back. You trust Jesus.

Justice changes how you treat other people

Micah 6:8 tells God's people to do justice, love mercy, and walk humbly with God.

Notice the balance:

- **Do justice** - stand for what is right.
- **Love mercy** - don't become cruel.
- **Walk humbly** - remember you need grace too.

Some people love "justice talk" but forget mercy. They become harsh and proud.

Others love "mercy talk" but forget justice. They excuse sin and call it love.

God calls you to both.

Real life: what justice looks like for a teen

Justice is not only big court cases and politics. It also hits school hallways and group chats.

Here are three places to practice justice with mercy:

1) In your friend group

If someone is being mocked, don't join in. Don't stay quiet to stay safe.

You don't have to be loud. You can be steady.

"Hey, stop. That's not okay."

2) In your words

Gossip feels small, but it damages people.

Justice means you don't use your mouth to harm someone made in God's image.

3) In your choices

Cheating is injustice. Lying is injustice. Taking what isn't yours is injustice.

God cares about the "small" wrongs too.

Quick check (answer in your own words)

1. What does it mean that God is just?

2. Why is God's patience not the same as God ignoring evil?

3. How does the cross show both justice and mercy?

4. What is one way you can do justice and love mercy this week?

Memory verse

*"He is the Rock, his works are perfect, and all his ways
are just. A faithful God who does no wrong, upright and
just is he.." — Deuteronomy 32:4*

Action step for the week

Do one "justice and mercy" action this week. Pick one:

✝ Apologize to someone you treated unfairly.

✝ Refuse to join in gossip and change the subject.

✝ Stand up for someone being targeted.

✝ Make something right if you took or damaged something.

✝ Tell the truth about a lie you told, even if it costs you.

Then write two lines after you do it:

✝ **Justice:** what was made right?

✝ **Mercy:** how did you stay kind and humble?

Closing prayer

Just God, thank You that You always do what is right. Forgive me for
my sin. Thank You for Jesus, who took my punishment. Help me love
what is right and hate what is evil. Help me treat people fairly and show
mercy like You have shown me. Amen.

WEEK 12
Remember God Never Changes:
God Is Faithful

People change.

Friends drift. Promises break. Plans fall apart. Even your own feelings can flip in one day.

So it's normal to wonder, "Can I really count on God?"

The Bible answers with a clear yes.

God is faithful. He keeps His word. He does not forget. He does not quit halfway. He does not get bored of you. He does not fail when life gets hard.

And when you are faithless, God stays faithful to His character.

The big idea

God is faithful, so you can trust His promises, keep going when you struggle, and return to Him when you fail.

Key Bible passages (read these first)

- **Lamentations 3:22-23** - God's mercies are new every morning.
- **2 Timothy 2:11-13** - God remains faithful even when we are faithless.
- **Numbers 23:19** - God does not lie or change His mind like humans.
- **1 Corinthians 1:9** - God is faithful and calls you into fellowship with Jesus.

What "God is faithful" means

God's faithfulness means:

- God keeps His promises.
- God does what He says.
- God finishes what He starts.
- God stays true to Himself.

God is not like a person who overpromises, then forgets.

When God commits, He commits fully.

Numbers 23:19 says God does not lie. He does not speak and then fail to act.

That means when God makes a promise, it is not a wish. It is certain.

Why this matters for teens

Teen years can feel shaky.

You're growing fast. Your friendships can change quickly. Your future can feel unclear. Your emotions can be loud.

In a season that moves, you need a foundation that doesn't move.

God's faithfulness is that foundation.

God's faithfulness does not mean life will be easy

Some people confuse faithfulness with comfort.

But faithfulness means God stays with you and keeps His word, even in hard seasons.

Lamentations 3 was written in a time of deep pain. The writer is not pretending everything is fine.

And yet he says: God's love and mercy are still there, and they are new each morning.

That is faithfulness: steady love in a messy world.

The strongest proof: God keeps His promises in Jesus

God promised a Savior long before Jesus was born.

Then, at the right time, Jesus came.

He lived the life we should live. He died for sinners. He rose again. He will return.

That's God's faithfulness in action.

So when you wonder, "Will God keep His promises to me?" look at what He already did for the world.

God is not guessing. He has a track record.

What about when you mess up?

This is where many teens feel stuck.

You sin, then you think: "God must be done with me."

But 2 Timothy 2:13 says: "If we are faithless, he remains faithful."

That does not mean sin is fine. It means God does not stop being God.

If you belong to Jesus, your hope is not your perfect record.

Your hope is God's faithful character and Jesus' finished work.

So what do you do after you mess up?

- Admit it to God.
- Turn from it.
- Trust Jesus again.
- Take the next right step.

Faithfulness means God meets you there, not that He excuses sin.

Faithfulness helps you handle doubt

Doubt often feels like a storm in your head.

Faithfulness gives you a steady truth: God is not changing every time you have a hard thought.

Some teens think faith means never questioning anything.

Better picture:Faith means bringing questions to God, not running away from Him.

You can say: "God, I'm struggling. Help me."

And keep walking.

Real life: where God's faithfulness meets you this week

Here are three moments where you can lean on God's faithfulness.

1) When you feel alone

God's faithfulness means He does not forget you.

He knows your name. He sees your life. He hears your prayers.

2) When you feel stuck in sin

God's faithfulness means you can repent and start again.

You are not trapped if you are in Christ.

3) When you're tired of trying

God's faithfulness means you can keep doing the right thing even when you don't feel strong.

Because your strength is not the main thing holding you.

God is.

Quick check (answer in your own words)

1. What does it mean that God is faithful?

   ----

2. How is God different from humans who break promises?

   ----

3. What does 2 Timothy 2:13 teach you about God when you fail?

   ----

4. What is one promise of God you need to trust this week?

Memory verse

"They are new every morning; great is your faithfulness."
- Lamentations 3:23

Action step for the week

Make a "promise list" you can return to.

1. Read these passages this week:
   - Day 1: Lamentations 3:22–26
   - Day 2: Psalm 23
   - Day 3: Romans 8:31–39
   - Day 4: John 10:27–30
   - Day 5: Philippians 1:6
   - Day 6: 1 Corinthians 10:13

2. Each day, write one line:

    o ____ "

God promises..." (write it in your own words)

____

____

____

____

____

____

3. At the end of the week, choose one promise and pray it every day
    for the next seven days.

Closing prayer

Faithful God, thank You for keeping Your word. Thank You for
staying steady when I change. Forgive me for the times I doubt You and
drift. Help me trust Your promises and keep walking with You. Thank
You for Jesus, who proves Your love. Amen.

WEEK 13
Worship the Trinity:
Father, Son, and Holy Spirit

If someone asks, "What do Christians believe about God?" the answer is not just, "God exists."

Christians believe something more specific:

There is one God, and He exists as three Persons: Father, Son, and Holy Spirit.

That's the Trinity.

It can sound confusing at first. But it's not a math trick. It's not "three gods." It's not "one god who changes masks."

It's God telling us who He is.

And it matters for real life because the Trinity is not a side topic. It shapes how you pray, how you trust Jesus, and how you understand love.

The big idea

God is one God in three Persons, so you can know God truly, worship Him rightly, and enjoy His saving work.

Key Bible passages (read these first)

- **Deuteronomy 6:4** — there is one God.
- **Matthew 28:18-20** — baptism in the name of the Father, Son, and Holy Spirit.
- **2 Corinthians 13:14** — Father, Son, and Spirit together in blessing.
- **John 1:1-3, 14** — the Son is God and became human.
- **Acts 5:3-4** — the Holy Spirit is God.

Start with what the Bible clearly teaches

Truth 1: There is one God

The Bible is not confused about this.

Deuteronomy 6:4 says the LORD is one.

Christians are not worshiping three gods. There is one God.

Truth 2: The Father is God

This is the easiest one for most people. The Father is called God many times.

Truth 3: The Son is God

John 1 says the Word was with God and was God, and the Word became flesh.

Jesus is not a created angel. He is not "a little god." He is fully God.

And Jesus receives worship (see Matthew 14:33). Only God should be worshiped.

Truth 4: The Holy Spirit is God

In Acts 5, lying to the Holy Spirit is described as lying to God.

The Spirit is not a force, not an energy, not "good vibes."

He is a Person who teaches, guides, convicts, and helps.

Truth 5: The Father, Son, and Spirit are distinct Persons

Jesus prays to the Father. The Father speaks about the Son. The Spirit is sent by the Father and the Son.

They are not the same Person pretending to be different.

So the Bible gives us a full picture:

- One God
- Three Persons
- Each Person is fully God
- The Persons are not each other

That is the Trinity.

Common mistakes to avoid

These show up online a lot, so it helps to name them.

Mistake 1: "Three gods"

That's not Christianity.

Christians believe in one God.

Mistake 2: "One Person who changes costumes"

Like God is the Father in the Old Testament, then becomes Jesus, then becomes the Spirit.

That fails because the Bible shows the Father, Son, and Spirit acting together at the same time.

Example: Jesus is baptized, the Spirit comes down, and the Father speaks (Matthew 3:16–17).

Mistake 3: "Jesus is less than God"

Some groups teach Jesus is a high created being.

But the Bible presents Jesus as truly God, worthy of worship, and eternal.

A simple way to say it (that stays faithful to Scripture)

Try this sentence:

The Trinity means one God exists forever as three distinct Persons: Father, Son, and Holy Spirit, equal in power and glory.

If you can say that clearly, you're doing well.

Why the Trinity matters in real life

1) It explains love

The Bible says God is love (1 John 4:8).

Love is not just a thing God started doing after He made people.

Before creation, the Father loved the Son (John 17:24). Love has always existed in God's own life.

That means love is not a human invention. It comes from God.

2) It explains salvation

Think about how God saves:

- The **Father** planned salvation and sent the Son.
- The **Son** came, lived, died, and rose again for sinners.
- The **Holy Spirit** applies salvation to you, gives you new life, and helps you grow.

If you remove the Trinity, the gospel starts falling apart.

3) It shapes your prayer

When you pray, you are not sending words into empty space.

You are coming to a real God.

A simple Bible pattern is:

✝ pray to the **Father,**

✝ through the **Son,**

✝ by the **Holy Spirit's** help.

That doesn't mean you can't pray to Jesus. Many prayers in Scripture are directed to Him. The point is: prayer is Trinitarian because God is Trinitarian.

Real life: how to relate to God this week

Here's a simple way to bring this home.

When you feel...

✝ **Guilty:** remember the **Son** paid for sin.

✝ **Alone:** remember the **Father** adopts you.

✝ **Weak:** remember the **Spirit** helps you obey.

You don't have to guess which "version" of God you're dealing with.

You're dealing with the one true God who saves.

Quick check (answer in your own words)

1. What are the five basic truths the Bible teaches that lead to the Trinity?

   ____

   ____

   ____

   ____

2. What is one common mistake people make about the Trinity?

   ____

   ____

   ____

   ____

3. How does the Trinity help you understand the gospel?

   ____

   ____

   ____

   ____

4. Which Person of the Trinity do you think about least, and why?

____

____

____

____

Memory verse

> *"Baptizing them in the name of the Father and of the Son
> and of the Holy Spirit." — Matthew 28:19*

Action step for the week

Pray one short Trinitarian prayer each day for 6 days.

Use this pattern:

- **Father:** thank You for_________________________________ .
- **Jesus:** thank You for dying and rising for _________________ .
- **Holy Spirit:** help me obey You today in___________________ .

Keep it specific and honest.

Example: "Father, thank You for caring for me today. Jesus, thank You for forgiving my sin. Holy Spirit, help me speak kindly at home."

Closing prayer

Father, thank You for sending Your Son. Jesus, thank You for saving me. Holy Spirit, thank You for helping me follow Christ. Help me worship You as You truly are. Keep my faith grounded in Your Word. Amen.

PART THREE
See Yourself Clearly

WEEK 14
Know Your Worth: Made in God's Image

A lot of teens live like their worth is a scoreboard.

- grades
- sports
- looks
- followers
- dating status
- being funny
- being noticed

When you win, you feel fine. When you lose, you feel small.

The Bible gives you something stronger than a scoreboard.

You are made in God's image.

That truth doesn't make you perfect. It does make you valuable. And it changes how you treat yourself and other people.

The big idea

Every person is made in God's image, so your life has real value, your choices matter, and you should treat others with honor.

Key Bible passages (read these first)

- **Genesis 1:26–28** - God makes humans in His image.
- **Genesis 9:6** - human life has value because of God's image.
- **Psalm 139:13–16** - God formed you on purpose.
- **James 3:9–10** - don't curse people made in God's likeness.

What does "image of God" mean?

It does not mean you look like God physically.

God is Spirit.

It means God made humans to **reflect** Him in special ways. You were made to show something of God's character in the world.

Here are four simple parts of what that includes.

1) You can know God

Animals can react and learn. Humans can pray, worship, and understand truth about God.

You were made for a relationship with Him.

2) You can think and choose

You can reason. You can plan. You can choose right or wrong.

That means your choices have weight. Your life isn't random.

3) You can love in a personal way

You can make promises. You can forgive. You can serve. You can build trust.

That kind of personal love reflects God.

4) You are meant to represent God's rule

Genesis 1 says humans are called to "rule" and "fill" the earth.

That doesn't mean people can do whatever they want. It means you are meant to care for God's world under God's authority.

So the image of God is not mainly about feeling special.

It's about being made for a purpose.

Your worth is real even when you feel low

Psalm 139 says God formed you. He saw your unformed body. Your days were written in His book.

That means you are not a mistake.

You might feel unwanted. You might feel awkward. You might feel behind.

But your worth is not built on your performance. It is built on God's design.

This matters especially when you feel shame.

Shame says, "I am trash."

God's Word says, "You are made in God's image, and you are still responsible for your sin."

Both can be true:

+ you are valuable,

+ and you need grace.

The image of God is in every person

This is huge.

Genesis 9:6 ties human life's value to God's image.

James 3 says it's wrong to praise God and then trash people with your mouth, because people are made in God's likeness.

So the image of God includes:

+ the kid everyone ignores,

+ the loud kid you can't stand,

+ the teacher who annoys you,

+ the person from a different background,

+ the person who hurt you.

This doesn't mean you trust unsafe people. It means you don't treat people like they're less than human.

A common question: "What about people with disabilities?"

Some people wrongly act like the image of God depends on ability.

But Scripture grounds human worth in God's creation, not in IQ, strength, or health.

A person's value doesn't shrink when their body or mind is weak.

This is one reason Christians care about the unborn, the elderly, the sick, and the overlooked.

How sin affects the image (but doesn't erase it)

Sin damages us. It twists how we reflect God.

But it does not erase the image of God.

That's why murder is wrong (Genesis 9). That's why slander is wrong (James 3). That's why humans still matter, even after the fall.

And it's why we need Jesus: to restore what sin has wrecked.

Jesus shows what the image of God looks like

If you want to see a human life that fully reflects God, look at Jesus.

Jesus is not only the Savior. He is also the perfect image of God.

He shows:

- ✝ truth without cruelty,
- ✝ strength without pride,
- ✝ holiness without coldness,
- ✝ love without lies.

Following Jesus is not just learning rules.

It's becoming more like the One who shows true humanity.

Real life: what this changes this week

1) How you talk to yourself

If you speak to yourself like you're worthless, you're agreeing with a lie.

You may need to repent of self-hate. It's not humility. It's distrust of God's design.

Try replacing "I'm a joke" with: "I'm made in God's image. I need help, and God gives help."

2) How you treat other people

Before you clap back, before you roast someone, before you spread a screenshot, remember:

That person is made in God's image.

Your words can either honor that or attack it.

3) How you use your body

Your body is not meaningless. It's not just a tool for pleasure or attention.

Because you belong to God, your body matters. You were made to honor Him.

Week 43 will go deeper on purity. This week is the foundation: your body is part of your God-given life.

Quick check (answer in your own words)

1. What does it mean to be made in God's image?

----

2. Name two ways humans reflect God differently than animals.

----

3. How should the image of God change how you treat people you dislike?

----

4. What is one lie about your worth that you need to reject?

Memory verse

"So God created mankind in his own image, in the image of God he created them; male and female he created them." - Genesis 1:27

Action step for the week

Do the "Image of God Practice" for 5 days.

Each day, write two lines:

1. **About me:** "Because I'm made in God's image, I will____today."

   (Example: "tell the truth," "work hard," "show respect," "stop trash talk.")

2. **About others:** "Because they're made in God's image, I will _________________________today."

   (Example: "stop gossip," "include someone," "apologize," "be patient.")

Then do one of the two lines the same day.

Closing prayer

God, thank You for making me on purpose. Forgive me for believing lies about my worth. Help me see myself and others the way You do. Help me honor Your image with my words, choices, and life. Amen.

WEEK 15
Face the Problem: What Sin Really Is

Most teens don't like the word "sin."

It can sound like an old insult. Or it can sound like, "You're bad, so feel guilty."

But the Bible uses the word "sin" because it tells the truth.

If you don't know what the problem is, you won't look for the right help.

And if you shrink sin down, you'll shrink Jesus down too.

Sin is not mainly "breaking rules."

Sin is turning from God.

The big idea

Sin is rebellion against God in our hearts and actions, so we must stop making excuses and turn to Jesus for forgiveness and change.

Key Bible passages (read these first)

- **Romans 3:10–12, 23** - everyone sins; no one is righteous.
- **1 John 1:8–10** - denying sin is self-deception; confession brings forgiveness.
- **James 1:14–15** - sin grows from desire to action to death.
- **Mark 7:20–23** - sin comes from the heart.

What sin is (in simple words)

Sin is:

- **wanting your way instead of God's way**
- **trusting yourself instead of trusting God**
- **loving what God hates**
- **ignoring what God commands**
- **putting something else in God's place**

Sin is not only what you do. It's also what you love, want, and chase.

That's why Jesus says evil comes from within (Mark 7).

You can look "fine" on the outside and still have a heart full of sin on the inside.

Three ways the Bible talks about sin

The Bible uses different pictures to help you see sin clearly.

1) Missing the mark

Like aiming at a target and falling short.

God's standard is perfect love for God and neighbor. We miss.

2) Breaking God's law

God gives commands because He is good. Sin breaks them.

This includes the obvious ones (lying, stealing) and the less "visible" ones (envy, pride).

3) Rebellion

This is the deepest one.

Sin is saying, "God, I know better."

That's why sin is serious. It's not only about behavior. It's about rejecting God's right to rule.

Sin starts in desire

James 1 shows a chain:

- desire pulls you
- sin is born
- sin grows
- it leads to death

This matters because you can't fight sin only at the "action" stage.

If you only say, "I won't do it," but you keep feeding the desire, you will keep falling.

You fight sin by dealing with what you want.

Example: If you keep feeding lust with videos, you will struggle more, not less.

If you keep feeding bitterness by replaying what someone did, anger will grow.

If you keep feeding pride by needing praise, you'll feel crushed when you're ignored.

Why teens make excuses for sin

Here are some common excuses. They sound normal, but they are lies.

- "Everyone does it."
- "It's not hurting anyone."
- "It's just how I am."
- "I had a hard day."
- "They started it."

Yes, life is hard. Yes, people hurt you. Yes, pressure is real.

But excuses keep you stuck.

God does not shame you to destroy you. He tells the truth to free you.

Two kinds of sin: what you do and what you fail to do

Most people think sin only means doing bad things.

But Scripture also talks about failing to do good.

- Not helping when you could.
- Not speaking truth when someone is being crushed.
- Not honoring your parents.
- Not praying when you're anxious.
- Not trusting God when you are scared.

Sin is not only ugly actions. It's also ignoring love.

The danger of comparing yourself

A teen might say: "I'm not perfect, but I'm not as bad as them."

Romans 3 shuts that down.

"All have sinned and fall short of the glory of God."

Comparison can make you proud or hopeless.

- Proud: "I'm better than others."
- Hopeless: "I can never change."
- The gospel gives you a better place:
- Honest about sin, hopeful in Christ.

The best news after the hard news

If you stop at sin, you'll feel crushed.

But the Bible does not stop there.

1 John 1 says if you confess, God forgives and cleanses.

That means you can be honest without fear.

You don't have to hide. You don't have to pretend. You don't have to cover it up.

Jesus is a real Savior for real sinners.

Real life: how to face sin this week

Facing sin is not about hating yourself.

It's about telling the truth, then turning to God.

Here's a simple pattern you can use:

1. **Name it** (no soft words)

    Not "I messed up." Say what it was: lying, lust, envy, hatred.

2. **Own it** (no blame)

    "I chose this."

3. **Confess it**

    Tell God the truth.

4. **Turn from it**

    Make one clear change: delete, block, apologize, set a boundary, ask for help.

5. **Trust Jesus**

    Don't stay in shame. Trust His forgiveness.

Quick check (answer in your own words)

1. What is sin, beyond breaking rules?

    ____

    ____

    ____

2. Where does sin come from, according to Mark 7?

    ____

    ____

    ____

3. What excuse do you use most often for sin?

    ____

    ____

    ____

4. What is one sin you need to confess and turn from this week?

____

____

____

____

Memory verse

"for all have sinned and fall short of the glory of God," -
Romans 3:23

Action step for the week

Do a "Truth and Turn" step one time this week.

1. Read **1 John 1:5–10**.
2. Write two lines:
     o **Truth:** "This week I sinned by _____________________."
     o **Turn:** "With God's help I will _____________________."
3. Do one clear action within 24 hours:
     o apologize to someone,
     o delete an app or account that feeds sin,
     o ask a trusted adult for help,
     o make a plan to avoid a repeated temptation.

If your sin is heavy or ongoing, don't carry it alone.

Closing prayer

God, thank You for telling the truth about my heart. Forgive me for my sin. Please help me stop making excuses. Thank You for Jesus who saves sinners. Help me turn from what is wrong and walk in Your light. Amen.

WEEK 16
Name the Damage:
What Sin Does to Us and Our World

Sin is not just "breaking rules."

Sin breaks people.

It breaks trust. It breaks families. It breaks minds. It breaks bodies. It breaks communities. It breaks your joy. It breaks your peace.

And sin doesn't only hurt the person who does it. It spills. It spreads. It leaves marks on others.

This week is about naming the damage so you stop treating sin like a small problem.

But we won't end in despair. The Bible never does.

We name the damage so we can run to the right rescue.

The big idea

Sin damages your relationship with God, your heart, your relationships, and the world, so you must take sin seriously and cling to Jesus for healing and hope.

Key Bible passages (read these first)

✝ **Genesis 3:1–24** - the first sin and its ripple effects.

✝ **Romans 6:23** - sin earns death.

✝ **Isaiah 59:1–2** - sin separates people from God.

✝ **Ephesians 2:1–5** - sin leaves us spiritually dead, but God gives life in Christ.

Start at the beginning: Genesis 3

Genesis 3 is not a "cute story." It explains why the world is the way it is.

Adam and Eve disobey God. Then what happens right away?

1) They hide from God

They feel shame and fear.

Sin changes how you see God.

Instead of running to Him, you run from Him.

2) They cover themselves

They feel exposed. They try to fix it with a quick cover.

Sin makes you try to save yourself.

You cover with:

- jokes
- "I'm fine"
- anger
- success
- looks
- being busy
- pretending you don't care

But covers don't heal.

3) They blame each other

Adam blames Eve. Eve blames the serpent.

Sin breaks honesty.

You stop saying, "I did wrong," and start saying, "Here's why it's not my fault."

4) The world gets cursed

Pain enters life in new ways. Work becomes frustrating. Relationships strain. Death becomes certain.

Sin doesn't stay in one corner. It spreads into everything.

Four big kinds of damage sin causes

Damage 1: Sin separates you from God

Isaiah 59 says sin creates a separation.

God is not distant because He is weak. He is holy.

Sin is not just "breaking a rule." It is breaking fellowship with the God who made you.

That's why sin often leads to spiritual dryness:

- you stop praying,
- you avoid Scripture,
- you start feeling numb.

Sin builds a wall, then tells you the wall is normal.

Damage 2: Sin twists your heart

Ephesians 2 says we were "dead" in sin.

That sounds harsh, but it explains something you already know:

You can't fix your deepest problem with willpower.

Sin doesn't only make you do bad things. It changes what you love.

It turns you inward.

It tells you:

- "Protect yourself first."
- "Get yours."
- "Use people."
- "Don't forgive."
- "Hold on to control."

And it trains your desires. What you feed grows.

Damage 3: Sin breaks relationships

Sin makes relationships hard because it produces things like:

- pride ("I'm right, you're wrong.")
- envy ("I hate your success.")
- lies ("I'll hide my real self.")
- lust ("I'll use you.")
- anger ("I'll punish you.")

Even "small" sins damage trust.

One lie can make a friend wonder what else is fake.

One cruel comment can stick for years.

One hidden habit can turn you into a double-life person.

Damage 4: Sin spreads into the world

Sin is personal, but it's also bigger than personal.

Human sin shapes cultures and systems and communities.

That's why we see:

- violence
- racism
- unfair courts
- abuse of power
- poverty caused by greed
- broken families

This does not mean every hard thing is caused by your personal sin.

But it does mean the world is broken because humanity is broken.

Sin leads to death

Romans 6:23 says, "The wages of sin is death."

Death is not only physical (though it is that).

Sin brings death-like things now too:

- dead joy
- dead peace
- dead trust
- dead hope
- dead relationships

Sin promises freedom and delivers chains.

It promises pleasure and delivers emptiness.

It promises control and delivers fear.

The enemy loves "soft" words for sin

Sin damage is easier to ignore when you rename it.

- "I'm just venting." (but it's gossip)
- "It's just a habit." (but it's addiction)
- "I'm just being honest." (but it's cruelty)
- "I'm just having fun." (but it's rebellion)

Soft words make sin feel safe.

God uses clear words because He wants real healing.

The hope: God moves toward sinners

Genesis 3 is full of bad news, but notice this:

God searches for Adam and Eve.

He asks questions, not because He doesn't know, but because He is drawing them out.

Then God gives a promise that points forward to a Rescuer (Genesis 3:15).

And God covers their shame with clothing, not fig leaves.

That's a sign: God provides what they could not provide.

The Bible keeps telling that story until Jesus comes and deals with sin fully.

Real life: what this changes for you

Here are three ways to apply this week.

1) Stop treating sin like a pet

Some sins feel "manageable" at first.

But sin grows.

If you feed it, it gets louder.

If you hide it, it gets stronger.

If you confess it, it loses power.

2) Look for the ripple

Ask:

- How is my sin affecting my family?
- How is it shaping my mind?
- How is it shaping how I treat people?

Sin always has a ripple, even when you can't see it right away.

3) Run to Jesus fast

When you sin, don't wait weeks to return to God.

Return quickly.

The longer you stay away, the more normal sin feels.

Quick check (answer in your own words)

1. Name two ways sin damaged life right after Genesis 3.

____

____

____

____

2. What does Isaiah 59 say sin does to your relationship with God?

----

3. How does sin harm relationships, even when it looks "small"?

----

4. What is one ripple effect of a sin you're tempted by?

Memory verse

"For the wages of sin is death, but the gift of God is eternal life in[a] Christ Jesus our Lord." - Romans 6:23

Action step for the week

Do the "Ripple Check" one time this week.

1. Write down one sin you're tempted by most (be honest).
2. Draw three arrows from it and label them:
   - **Me** (how it affects your mind, joy, peace, or habits)
   - **Others** (how it affects friends, family, church)
   - **God** (how it affects prayer, trust, obedience)
3. Then write one "cut it off" step you will take in the next 24 hours. Examples:
   - talk to a trusted adult,
   - block a source of temptation,
   - apologize,
   - set a boundary for your phone at night,
   - leave a chat that pulls you into sin.

One step done today beats ten plans for later.

Closing prayer

God, please help me see sin the way You see it. I confess that sin damages my heart and my relationships. Forgive me through Jesus. Help me turn away from what destroys and walk in Your light. Give me strength to take one real step this week. Amen.

WEEK 17
Own Your Need:
Why You Can't Save Yourself

Most teens don't say, "I'm my own savior."

But a lot of teens live like it.

You try to fix yourself with:

- better habits
- more effort
- being nicer
- staying busy
- looking strong
- staying in control

And when you fail, you either hide it or hate yourself.

This week is a hard truth, but it's also one of the most freeing truths in the Bible:

You can't save yourself.

That's not an insult. It's a rescue sign.

The big idea

You can't save yourself because sin is deeper than effort, so your only hope is God's grace through Jesus Christ.

Key Bible passages (read these first)

- **Ephesians 2:1-10** - dead in sin, saved by grace, created for good works.
- **Romans 3:20-24** - no one is made right by works; we are justified by grace.
- **Titus 3:3-7** - saved not by our works but by God's mercy.
- **Luke 18:9-14** - the Pharisee and the tax collector.

Why you can't save yourself (three clear reasons)

1) Sin is not only "what you do," it's what you are

Ephesians 2 says we were "dead" in sin.

Dead people don't need advice. They need life.

That verse does not mean you are as evil as you could possibly be. It means sin has affected every part of you: mind, desires, choices.

So you can't fix your heart by trying harder, because your heart is part of the problem.

2) God's standard is perfect righteousness

Romans 3 says no one will be made right with God by works of the law.

Why?

Because God is holy.

If the standard is "mostly good," then many people might pass.

But the standard is love God fully and obey Him truly.

That leaves everyone short.

This is why comparing yourself to others is useless.

God's standard is not "better than your classmates."

It's perfect righteousness.

3) Good works can't erase guilt

Even if you start doing better today, what about yesterday?

Imagine you break a window, then mow the lawn to be "nice."

Mowing doesn't pay for the window.

Good works are good. But they don't erase guilt.

Sin has a debt. You can't pay it with kindness points.

A story Jesus told that makes this simple

Luke 18 shows two men praying.

One is a Pharisee. He lists his good works and thanks God that he's not like other people.

The other is a tax collector. He won't even lift his eyes. He says:

"God, be merciful to me, a sinner!"

Jesus says the second man went home made right with God.

Why?

Because God saves people who stop pretending.

The Pharisee trusted himself.

The tax collector trusted God's mercy.

This is where teens often get stuck

Some teens hear "you can't save yourself" and think:

"So I don't have to obey."

That's not the point.

The point is the order:

- ✝ You are **saved by grace.**
- ✝ Then you **obey from a new heart.**

Ephesians 2 says we are saved by grace through faith, not by works.

Then it says we are created in Christ for good works.

So good works are not the root of salvation.

They are the fruit.

What God does that you can't do

Titus 3 says God saves us by mercy, by washing and renewal.

That means God does the deep work:

- ✝ He forgives guilt.
- ✝ He gives you new life.
- ✝ He gives His Spirit.
- ✝ He changes you over time.

Christianity is not self-improvement.

It's salvation.

Real life: what this means for you this week

Here are three ways this truth helps in normal teen life.

1) When you feel proud

If you think you're "good enough," you'll look down on others.

This week reminds you: you are saved only by grace.

Grace kills pride.

2) When you feel crushed

If you think salvation depends on your performance, you'll live stressed.

Grace gives peace.

You don't have to earn God's love in Christ.

3) When you keep falling into the same sin

Trying harder is not always the answer.

Sometimes the answer is:

- confess,
- ask for help,
- set boundaries,
- and depend on Jesus daily.

You need more than effort. You need power from God.

Quick check (answer in your own words)

1. Why can't you save yourself? Give one clear reason.

2. What is wrong with trusting your good works to make you right with God?

3. In Luke 18, what made the tax collector different from the Pharisee?

4. Where do you most act like you have to "earn" God's love?

Memory verse

*"For it is by grace you have been saved, through faith—
and this is not from yourselves, it is the gift of God— not
by works, so that no one can boast." - Ephesians 2:8–9*

Action step for the week

Do the "Grace Reset" for 6 days.

Each day, read **Ephesians 2:1–10** (yes, the same passage).

Then write three short lines:

1. **I was...** (pick one phrase from verses 1–3 that fits the human problem)

2. **But God...** (pick one phrase from verses 4–7 that shows God's mercy)

3. **So now I will...** (pick one good work from verse 10 you can do today)

Example:

† I was: "following my own desires."

† But God: "made us alive with Christ."

† So now I will: "tell the truth today and apologize if needed."

Closing prayer

God, I admit I can't save myself. Forgive me for trusting my effort and my image. Thank You for Your grace in Jesus. Please give me a new heart and help me obey You from love, not fear. Amen.

PART FOUR
Follow Jesus for Real

WEEK 18
Meet the Promised King: Why Jesus Had to Come

If you only think of Jesus as a "nice teacher," the Bible won't make sense.

Why would a teacher need to be born from a virgin? Why would He be called "Lord"? Why would He be crucified? Why would His resurrection be the center of everything?

Jesus did not come mainly to give better tips for life.

Jesus came because something was broken that you could not fix.

Jesus had to come because God promised a Savior, sin brought real guilt, and only a true King could rescue and restore.

The big idea

Jesus had to come because God promised a Rescuer, humans are trapped in sin, and only Christ can bring forgiveness, a new heart, and God's kingdom.

Key Bible passages (read these first)

- ✝ **Genesis 3:15** - the first promise of a coming Rescuer.
- ✝ **Isaiah 9:6–7** - a King who will rule forever.
- ✝ **Micah 5:2** - the promised ruler from Bethlehem.
- ✝ **Luke 4:16–21** - Jesus says the promise is being fulfilled in Him.
- ✝ **Mark 10:45** - Jesus came to serve and give His life as a ransom.

Reason 1: God promised a Rescuer from the beginning

Right after sin enters the world in Genesis 3, God gives a promise.

Genesis 3:15 speaks of an offspring who will defeat the serpent, even though the serpent will strike him.

That is a seed of hope planted in the darkest moment.

From that point on, the Old Testament keeps pointing forward.

God keeps saying, in different ways: "I will send the One."

So Jesus didn't show up randomly.

He came as the promised answer.

Reason 2: Sin brought guilt and separation that we can't erase

Week 15–17 showed this:

- sin is rebellion,
- sin damages everything,
- and you can't save yourself.

That means the problem is not only "people need better morals."

The problem is:

- guilt before a holy God,
- hearts that love the wrong things,
- and death that no one can stop.

A good teacher can guide you.

A teacher cannot erase guilt.

A teacher cannot give you a new heart.

A teacher cannot defeat death.

So Jesus came as more than a teacher. He came as Savior.

Reason 3: God's justice must be satisfied

God is loving, but He is also just.

If God ignored evil, He would not be good.

So how can sinners be forgiven?

This is where Jesus "had to come."

Only Jesus could:

- live without sin,
- stand in the place of sinners,
- take the judgment sin deserves,
- and bring peace with God.

A sinful person can't pay for their own sin and then pay for others too.

Only the sinless Son could do that.

Reason 4: God's kingdom needed a true King

The Bible is not mainly the story of humans climbing up to God.

It's the story of God coming down to rescue.

And it's also the story of a King bringing His kingdom.

Isaiah 9 promises a King whose rule will never end.

This King won't just fix a few problems. He will bring a new kind of life under God's rule.

That's why Jesus' message often sounded like: "The kingdom of God is at hand."

He wasn't only offering forgiveness. He was calling people into a new life under God's reign.

Jesus fulfills promise after promise

Here are a few examples Scripture points to:

- **Born in Bethlehem** (Micah 5:2; fulfilled in the Gospels)
- **A descendant of David** (2 Samuel 7; Isaiah 9; fulfilled in Jesus' line)
- **A suffering servant** (Isaiah 53 points to suffering that brings healing and forgiveness)
- **A righteous King** whose reign brings peace (Isaiah 9)

You don't need to memorize a list today. The point is this:

Jesus fits the promises like a key fits a lock.

What Jesus came to do (in one sentence)

Mark 10:45 is one of the clearest summaries.

Jesus came:

- to serve,
- to give His life,
- as a ransom for many.

A ransom is a payment to set someone free.

That means sin is not just "oops."

Sin is slavery.

And Jesus came to purchase freedom.

Real life: why this matters for you now

If Jesus had to come, then Christianity is not mainly "try harder."

It's "trust the Rescuer."

Here's what that changes:

1) You don't have to hide your need

If Jesus came for sinners, then you don't have to pretend you're fine.
You can be honest.

2) You can stop chasing fake saviors

Teens often chase salvation in other places:

- being liked
- being wanted
- being impressive
- being in control
- being "good enough"

Those things can't save you. They can only demand more.

Jesus is the promised King who saves without using you.

3) Your life has a center

If Jesus is the promised King, then your life isn't about "finding yourself" first.

It's about knowing Him, following Him, and becoming who you were made to be.

Quick check (answer in your own words)

1. Why did Jesus have to come? Give one reason.

    ____

    ____

    ____

2. What promise in the Old Testament points to Jesus? Name one from this lesson.

    ____

    ____

    ____

3. Why can't a "good teacher" solve the deepest human problem?

    ____

    ____

    ____

4. What is one "fake savior" you're tempted to trust instead of Jesus?

____

____

____

____

Memory verse

"For even the Son of Man came not to be served but to serve, and to give his life as a ransom for many." -
Mark 10:45

Action step for the week

Do the "Promise and Fulfillment" practice 4 times this week.

Pick one pair each day:

- ✝ Day 1: **Micah 5:2** → read **Luke 2:1-7**
- ✝ Day 2: **Isaiah 9:6-7** → read **Luke 1:26-33**
- ✝ Day 3: **Isaiah 53:4-6** → read **Mark 15:15-39**
- ✝ Day 4: **Genesis 3:15** → read **Hebrews 2:14-18**

For each day, write:

- ✝ **Promise:** (one sentence)
- ✝ **Fulfillment:** (one sentence)
- ✝ **So I will:** (one response)

Closing prayer

God, thank You for keeping Your promises. Thank You for sending Jesus when I could not save myself. Help me trust Him as my Savior and King. Help me stop trusting fake saviors. Teach me to follow Christ with a willing heart. Amen.

WEEK 19
Hold Two Truths:
Jesus Is Fully God and Fully Man

Some people talk about Jesus like He was only a great human.

Others talk about Him like He was God pretending to be human.

The Bible won't let you pick just one.

It teaches two truths at the same time:

- † Jesus is fully God.
- † Jesus is fully man.

If you drop either truth, the gospel starts breaking.

This week helps you hold both truths without getting lost.

The big idea

Jesus is fully God and fully man, so He can reveal God perfectly, represent humans truly, and save sinners completely.

Key Bible passages (read these first)

- † **John 1:1–3, 14** - the Son is God and became flesh.
- † **Colossians 2:9** - all God's fullness dwells in Christ.
- † **Hebrews 2:14–18** - Jesus became human to help humans.
- † **Philippians 2:5–11** - Jesus humbled Himself and is exalted as Lord.
- † **Luke 2:52** - Jesus grew in wisdom and stature (real humanity).

Truth 1: Jesus is fully God

The Bible says Jesus is not "part God."

He is God.

John 1 says the Word was with God and was God.

Colossians 2 says the fullness of deity lives in Him.

That means Jesus has God's power, God's holiness, God's authority, and God's worth.

So Jesus can do things only God can do:

- ✝ forgive sins (Mark 2:5–12)
- ✝ calm storms with a word
- ✝ receive worship
- ✝ claim "I and the Father are one" (John 10:30)

If Jesus is not God, then:

- ✝ His words are not final,
- ✝ His cross can't save the world,
- ✝ and worshiping Him would be wrong.

But the Bible teaches He is worthy of worship.

Truth 2: Jesus is fully man

Jesus did not float around like a ghost.

He was born. He grew. He got tired. He ate. He slept. He felt sorrow. He wept. He suffered.

Luke 2:52 says He grew in wisdom and stature.

Hebrews 2 says He shared in flesh and blood.

That means Jesus is not acting human.

He is truly human.

If Jesus is not human, then:

- ✝ He can't stand in our place,
- ✝ He can't obey as a real human,
- ✝ and He can't die (because God cannot die).

But Jesus did die in His human nature.

One Person, two natures

Here's the careful way Christians have spoken for a long time:

Jesus is **one Person** with **two natures:**

- ✝ truly God
- ✝ truly man

Not half and half.

Not mixed into something new.

Not split into two people.

One Jesus.

This matters because it protects the Bible's teaching.

Why both truths matter for salvation

1) Only God can save

Saving sinners is not a small job.

Sin is against God. Death is real. Satan is real. God's justice is real.

Only God has the power and authority to rescue.

If Jesus is God, He can truly save.

2) Only a true human can stand in for humans

God's justice requires a real human obedience where humans failed.

Jesus obeyed in our place.

He became like us so He could represent us.

Hebrews 2 says He became human so He could be a merciful and faithful high priest and help those who are tempted.

That means Jesus doesn't save you from far away.

He saves you as the One who stepped into your world.

How Jesus being fully human helps your daily life

Some teens think:

"Jesus doesn't get it."

But Hebrews says He does.

Jesus understands:

- pressure
- temptation
- rejection
- grief
- tiredness
- loneliness

He faced temptation, yet He did not sin.

So when you're tempted, you're not praying to a distant force.

You're coming to a Savior who knows what temptation feels like, and who can help you stand.

How Jesus being fully God helps your daily life

Jesus is not only sympathetic.

He is strong.

If Jesus is God, then:

- His promises are solid.
- His forgiveness is real.
- His rule is unbreakable.
- His help is powerful.

When your life feels weak, you need more than empathy.

You need power.

Jesus gives both.

A common confusion: "Did Jesus stop being God?"

No.

Philippians 2 teaches that Jesus humbled Himself, but it does not say He stopped being God.

He didn't lose His deity.

He took on humanity and lived in humble obedience.

He chose the path of suffering, not the path of showing off His power.

That's why His humility is so beautiful.

Real life: holding both truths when you pray

Try these two lines in prayer this week:

- "Jesus, You are God. You are able."
- "Jesus, You became man. You understand."

Both are true.

And both should shape your trust.

Quick check (answer in your own words)

1. What does it mean that Jesus is fully God?

____

____

____

____

2. What does it mean that Jesus is fully man?

____

____

____

3. Why do we need both truths for salvation?

____

____

____

4. In your life right now, do you need Jesus' power or Jesus' compassion more? Explain.

____

____

____

Memory verse

"In him the whole fullness of deity dwells bodily." —
Colossians 2:9

Action step for the week

Do the "Two Truths" practice for 5 days.

Each day:

1. Read one passage:
   - Day 1: John 1:1–14
   - Day 2: Philippians 2:5–11
   - Day 3: Hebrews 2:14–18
   - Day 4: Luke 2:41–52
   - Day 5: Colossians 1:15–20

2. Write two short lines:
   - **Fully God:** what this passage shows about Jesus' deity
   - **Fully Man:** what this passage shows about Jesus' humanity

3. Pray one sentence:

   "Jesus, help me trust You today because You are __________."

Closing prayer

Lord Jesus, thank You for becoming human for me. Thank You for being fully God, able to save. Help me trust You when I'm tempted and tired. Help me worship You with joy and live under Your care. Amen.

WEEK 20
Watch Jesus Up Close:
What His Life Shows About God

Some teens picture God as distant.

Others picture Him as angry.

Others picture Him as a "good vibes" helper.

Jesus clears the fog.

If you want to know what God is like, look at Jesus. He is God the Son living among us. His life shows God's character in a way you can see.

Jesus didn't only teach truth. He showed truth with His actions.

The big idea

Jesus shows you what God is like, so you can trust God's character and follow Christ with real faith.

Key Bible passages (read these first)

- ✝ **John 14:8–11** - Jesus says He reveals the Father.
- ✝ **Colossians 1:15–20** - Jesus is the image of the invisible God.
- ✝ **Mark 1:35–39** - Jesus prays and stays focused on His mission.
- ✝ **Mark 2:1–12** - Jesus forgives sins and proves His authority.
- ✝ **John 11:32–44** - Jesus weeps, then raises Lazarus.

What Jesus' life shows about God

1) God is near to the weak and hurting

Jesus moved toward people others avoided.

He touched lepers. He welcomed children. He spoke with outcasts. He cared for the poor and rejected.

This is not God being soft about sin. It is God being kind to sinners who know they need help.

Real life: When you feel ashamed, Jesus shows God is not scared of your mess.

2) God tells the truth, even when it costs

Jesus never lied to keep peace.

He corrected pride. He exposed fake religion. He warned about judgment. He spoke plainly about sin.

Jesus' truth was never meant to crush. It was meant to rescue.

Real life: If you follow Jesus, you can't build your life on pretending.

3) God has authority over sin, sickness, and storms

In Mark 2, Jesus forgives a man's sins.

People are shocked because only God can forgive sins.

Then Jesus heals the man to prove His authority is real.

Real life: Jesus is not a helpful life coach. He is Lord with power to save.

4) God is compassionate, not cold

In John 11, Jesus sees grief and weeps.

Then He raises Lazarus.

He cares, and He acts.

Real life: God is not annoyed by tears. He is present in sorrow.

5) God is holy and hates evil

Jesus was gentle, but He was never casual about sin.

He called people to repent. He warned about hell. He cleaned out the temple.

His holiness was not harsh. It was clean.

Real life: Jesus is kind enough to forgive you and strong enough to change you.

6) God obeys God's Word and depends on God in prayer

Jesus prayed often.

Mark 1 shows Jesus rising early to pray. He also faced pressure and did not let crowds control His mission.

This shows something important: perfect human life is not "independent life." It is dependent life.

Real life: If Jesus prayed, you need prayer too.

One simple rule for reading the Gospels

When you read about Jesus, watch for three things:

- ✝ **What He says** (His truth)
- ✝ **What He does** (His power and mercy)
- ✝ **What He loves** (His priorities)

Then ask one direct question: **What does this show me about God's character?**

Answer it from the passage, not from your mood.

Common mistake: loving a "half Jesus"

Some people want Jesus as a friend but not a King.

Others want Jesus as a powerful leader but not a gentle Savior.

The Gospels don't give you a half Jesus.

They show one Jesus:

- ✝ full of grace and truth,
- ✝ strong and gentle,
- ✝ holy and welcoming.

If your Jesus never corrects you, that isn't the Bible's Jesus.

If your Jesus never comforts you, that isn't the Bible's Jesus either.

Real life: what this changes for you this week

Here are three places to apply what you see in Jesus.

1) Your view of God

Don't guess what God is like. Look at Jesus.

When you're tempted to think, "God doesn't care," remember Jesus weeping at Lazarus' tomb.

2) Your view of yourself

Jesus moved toward needy people.

So you don't need to clean yourself up first. You come to Him, confess, and trust Him.

3) Your view of others

If Jesus treated people with patience and truth, you should too.

That doesn't mean you accept sin. It means you speak truth with love.

Quick check (answer in your own words)

1. What does Jesus show you about God that you forget most often?

   ____

   ____

   ____

   ____

2. Name one story from this week's readings that helped you.

   ____

   ____

   ____

   ____

3. How does Jesus treat sinners who come to Him honestly?

   ____

   ____

   ____

   ____

4. What is one way you can copy Jesus' compassion this week?

   ____

   ____

   ____

   ____

Memory verse

"Jesus answered: "Don't you know me, Philip, even after I have been among you such a long time? Anyone who has seen me has seen the Father. How can you say, 'Show us the Father'?" - John 14:9

Action step for the week

Do a "Gospel Close-Up" for 5 days.

Each day:

1. Read one passage:
   - Day 1: Mark 2:1–12
   - Day 2: Mark 4:35–41
   - Day 3: Mark 5:21–43

- o Day 4: John 11:32-44
- o Day 5: John 13:1-17

2. Write three short lines:
   - o God is ________________________________
   - o Jesus shows this by ________________________________
   - o So I will ________________________________

Keep it simple. One sentence each.

Closing prayer

Lord Jesus, thank You for showing me what God is like. Help me trust Your heart and Your authority. Help me follow You with honesty and courage. Make my life look more like Yours. Amen.

WEEK 21
Understand the Cross:
What Jesus Achieved

The cross is the center of Christianity.

Not a side symbol. Not just a sad ending.

If you miss what Jesus did on the cross, you miss the gospel.

Many people think the cross means, "God loves me," and that's true.

But it means more than that.

The cross is where Jesus paid for sin, satisfied God's justice, defeated evil, and opened the way for you to be forgiven and changed.

The big idea

Jesus' cross paid for sin and made peace with God, so you can be forgiven, freed from guilt, and live a new life with hope.

Key Bible passages (read these first)

- **Isaiah 53:4-6** - the servant bears our sin.
- **Mark 15:33-39** - Jesus' death.
- **2 Corinthians 5:21** - Jesus takes our sin; we receive His righteousness.
- **1 Peter 2:24** - Jesus bore our sins so we could live for righteousness.
- **Colossians 2:13-15** - forgiveness and victory over evil powers.

Start with the problem the cross solves

Week 15-17 taught the problem clearly:

- God is holy.
- God is just.
- you and I sin.
- we can't erase guilt.
- we can't save ourselves.

So the question becomes:

How can a holy God forgive guilty people and still be just?

The cross answers that.

What Jesus achieved on the cross (five clear truths)

1) Jesus took our punishment

Isaiah 53 says He was pierced for our transgressions and crushed for our iniquities.

That means Jesus didn't die for His own sins.

He died for ours.

This is called substitution: Jesus stood in the place of sinners.

Real life: When guilt screams, you can answer, "Jesus paid for that."

2) Jesus satisfied God's justice

God does not ignore evil. He judges it.

At the cross, God's justice fell on sin; on Jesus, who carried sin.

So forgiveness is not God pretending sin is fine.

Forgiveness is God dealing with sin fully, then offering mercy to those who trust Christ.

Real life: You don't have to wonder if God is still angry at you every time you fail. If you are in Christ, sin has been judged.

3) Jesus removed your guilt and shame

2 Corinthians 5:21 says God made Him who knew no sin to be sin for us, so we could become the righteousness of God in Him.

That means:

✝ your sin is credited to Jesus,

✝ His righteousness is credited to you.

So God doesn't treat you like you're "almost clean."

In Christ, you are accepted.

Real life: Shame says, "You are your sin." The cross says, "Your sin is paid for, and you belong to Jesus."

4) Jesus broke sin's power

1 Peter 2:24 says Jesus bore our sins so that we might die to sin and live to righteousness.

That means the cross is not only about a future home in heaven.

It's about real change now.

You won't become sinless overnight, but you can grow.

Real life: You can say no to sin because you're not trapped the way you were.

5) Jesus defeated the enemy's claim

Colossians 2 says Jesus canceled the record of debt and disarmed rulers and authorities.

One way to say it simply:

The enemy loves to accuse you. The cross removes the weapon of accusation.

If the debt is canceled, the enemy has no legal claim.

Real life: When you're tempted to think, "God could never want me," remember: the cross is louder than the accusation.

What the cross does not mean

Let's clear two mistakes.

Mistake 1: "Jesus died so I can sin and still be fine"

No.

The cross saves you from sin, not for sin.

If you use grace as an excuse, you're missing grace.

Mistake 2: "I have to pay God back"

No.

You can't pay God back.

Jesus said, "It is finished" (John 19:30).

Your obedience is not repayment.

Your obedience is grateful love.

The cross and your everyday life

The cross changes how you live Monday to Friday.

1) It changes how you handle failure

You don't hide.

You confess fast.

You return to God because you know forgiveness is real.

2) It changes how you treat others

If you've been forgiven, you can forgive.

This doesn't mean you ignore abuse or stay in unsafe situations.

It means you don't build your life on revenge.

3) It changes how you face fear

If Jesus loved you enough to die for you, He won't abandon you now.

Quick check (answer in your own words)

1. Why did Jesus have to die?

   ____

   ____

   ____

   ____

2. What does it mean that Jesus took our place?

   ____

   ____

   ____

   ____

3. Which part of the cross do you need most right now: forgiveness, freedom from shame, strength to change, or hope?

   ____

   ____

   ____

   ____

4. What is one lie about the cross you've heard or believed?

   ____

   ____

   ____

   ____

Memory verse

"He himself bore our sins" in his body on the cross, so that we might die to sins and live for righteousness; "by his wounds you have been healed." - 1 Peter 2:24

Action step for the week

Do the "Cross Truth" practice for 5 days.

Each day:

1. Read one passage:
    - o   Day 1: Isaiah 53:4–6
    - o   Day 2: Mark 15:33–39
    - o   Day 3: 2 Corinthians 5:17–21
    - o   Day 4: 1 Peter 2:21–25
    - o   Day 5: Colossians 2:13–15

2. Write two lines:
    - o   **Jesus achieved:** (one clear truth from the passage)
    - o   **So today I will:** (one response: confess, forgive, resist sin, worship, obey)

Closing prayer

Lord Jesus, thank You for the cross. Thank You for taking my place and paying for my sin. Help me stop living in guilt and shame. Help me trust Your finished work and walk in new obedience. Amen.

WEEK 22
Trust the Resurrection:
Why It Matters Today

If Jesus stayed dead, Christianity falls apart.

No resurrection means:

- no victory,
- no real forgiveness,
- no living Savior,
- no future hope.

But the Bible claims something bold: **Jesus rose from the dead.**

Not as a symbol. Not as a "spiritual idea." As a real event in history.

And it matters for your life today, not just for your future.

The big idea

Jesus rose from the dead, so your faith is grounded in truth, your sin is forgiven, your future is secure, and your life can change right now.

Key Bible passages (read these first)

- **Luke 24:1-12** - the empty tomb.
- **1 Corinthians 15:3-8, 12-20** - the gospel and why the resurrection matters.
- **Romans 6:4-11** - raised life means new life now.
- **1 Peter 1:3** - living hope through the resurrection.

What the resurrection is

The resurrection means Jesus truly died, then truly rose with a real body.

He wasn't a ghost.

He ate with people. He talked with them. He could be touched. He was recognized.

And yet His body was also changed; no longer under the power of death.

So the resurrection is not "Jesus' ideas lived on."

It is God raising Jesus from the grave.

Why the resurrection matters (five strong reasons)

1) It proves Jesus is who He said He is

Many people claim to speak for God.

Only Jesus rose from the dead.

The resurrection is God's public "yes" to Jesus' identity and mission.

Real life: You can trust Jesus' words because God confirmed Him.

2) It means the cross worked

1 Corinthians 15 says if Christ has not been raised, your faith is empty and you are still in your sins.

That's direct.

The resurrection shows that sin was paid for and death was defeated.

Real life: You don't have to wonder if God really forgives. The empty tomb is God's answer.

3) It gives you living hope

1 Peter 1:3 says God gave us new birth into a living hope through Jesus' resurrection.

"Living hope" is not wishful thinking.

It is confidence that God will keep His promise, even if life is hard right now.

Real life: Your worst day is not the end of your story.

4) It means Jesus is alive and active now

Jesus is not a memory.

He reigns now.

He hears prayer. He helps His people. He builds His church.

Real life: You are not praying to a dead hero. You are praying to a living Lord.

5) It means you can live a new life now

Romans 6 says we were united with Christ in His death and resurrection.

So the resurrection is not only about heaven later.

It's about change now:

- new desires,
- new strength,
- new direction.

Real life: You can fight sin with hope because the power of new life is real.

A key truth: the resurrection doesn't remove all pain yet

Some teens think, "If Jesus rose, why do Christians still suffer?"

Because we live in the "already and not yet."

Already:

- Jesus has risen,
- sin has been paid for,
- the kingdom has begun.

Not yet:

- the world is still broken,
- bodies still get sick,
- death still happens.

But the resurrection promises a future where death is finished for good.

So Christians grieve, but not like people with no hope.

How to respond when someone says, "Dead people don't rise"

That's true by normal nature.

That's the point.

The resurrection is a miracle. It is not "nature doing its usual thing."

Christianity is claiming God acted in history.

So the question becomes: If God exists, can He raise the dead?

If God made life, He can restore life.

Real life: how the resurrection shapes your week

Here are three ways to live resurrection faith as a teen.

1) When you feel stuck

Resurrection means God brings life where there was death.

So don't say, "I'll never change."

Say, "Jesus is alive, so change is possible."

Then take one real step: confess, ask for help, set a boundary, obey.

2) When you feel afraid

Fear often says, "What if everything falls apart?"

Resurrection says, "Even death doesn't win."

That doesn't remove all anxiety fast, but it gives you a deeper ground under your feet.

3) When you feel alone

A living Savior means you are not abandoned.

Jesus is with His people. He keeps His promises.

Quick check (answer in your own words)

1. Why does Christianity depend on the resurrection?

---

2. What does 1 Corinthians 15 say would be true if Jesus didn't rise?

---

3. What is "living hope," and how is it different from wishful thinking?

---

4. Where do you need resurrection hope most right now: fear, shame, or temptation?

Memory verse

"And if Christ has not been raised, your faith is futile; you are still in your sins." - 1 Corinthians 15:17

Action step for the week

Do the "Resurrection Response" for 5 days.

Each day:

1. Read a short passage:
   - Day 1: Luke 24:1-12
   - Day 2: Luke 24:36-49
   - Day 3: 1 Corinthians 15:3-8
   - Day 4: Romans 6:4-11
   - Day 5: 1 Peter 1:3-9
2. Write two lines:
   - Because Jesus is alive... (one truth)
   - Today I will... (one action that matches hope)

Examples:

- "Because Jesus is alive, I will confess my sin instead of hiding."
- "Because Jesus is alive, I will forgive instead of feeding bitterness."
- "Because Jesus is alive, I will keep praying."

Closing prayer

Lord Jesus, thank You that You rose from the dead. Help me trust that this is true. Give me living hope. Help me fight sin with courage and live like You are alive and near. Amen.

WEEK 23
Live Under His Rule:
Jesus Is Lord Right Now

Some people treat Jesus like a helper.

They want Him close when life hurts, but quiet when He gives commands.

But Jesus is not only Savior. He is Lord.

That word "Lord" means King, ruler, the One in charge.

And here's the truth that changes everything:

Jesus is Lord right now.

Not later. Not only in heaven. Right now.

That means following Jesus is not only believing facts. It is living under His rule.

The big idea

Jesus is Lord right now, so you should trust Him, obey Him, and live every part of life under His authority.

Key Bible passages (read these first)

- **Matthew 28:18–20** - Jesus has all authority.
- **Acts 2:32–36** - God made Jesus both Lord and Christ.
- **Philippians 2:9–11** - every knee will bow to Jesus.
- **Colossians 1:13–18** - Jesus rules over His kingdom and His church.

What it means to say "Jesus is Lord"

It means at least three things:

1) Jesus has authority over everyone and everything

Matthew 28:18 says Jesus has all authority in heaven and on earth.

Not some authority. All.

So Jesus is not one option on your shelf.

He is the rightful King over your life.

2) Jesus deserves your trust and worship

If Jesus is Lord, you don't treat Him like a myth or a motivational quote.

You worship Him because He is worthy.

Worship is not only singing. It's choosing His way because you believe He's good.

3) Jesus calls for obedience

Calling Jesus "Lord" but refusing His commands doesn't make sense.

Jesus said, "Why do you call me 'Lord, Lord,' and not do what I tell you?" (Luke 6:46)

So lordship is not mainly a label. It's a life direction.

Lordship does not mean your life becomes perfect

Following Jesus doesn't erase:

- stress,
- temptation,
- suffering,
- rejection.

But it does change who leads your life.

You stop living under:

- fear,
- peer pressure,
- anger,
- lust,
- pride,
- approval seeking.

And you learn to live under Christ.

A simple way to see it: two kingdoms

Colossians 1 says God delivered believers from the domain of darkness and transferred them to the kingdom of His beloved Son.

That means there are two ways to live:

✝ **Darkness kingdom:** "I'm in charge. I do what I want."

✝ **Jesus' kingdom:** "Jesus is in charge. I follow Him."

Being a Christian means you changed kingdoms.

So you can't say, "Jesus saved me," and then keep living like you're still the king.

What Jesus' rule looks like in teen life

This is where it gets real.

If Jesus is Lord, He has a claim on:

1) Your private life

Not just what people see.

✝ what you watch

✝ what you click

✝ what you hide

✝ what you think about late at night

Jesus' rule reaches the secret places.

Not to shame you, but to free you.

2) Your relationships

Jesus is Lord over:

✝ how you date,

✝ how you treat friends,

✝ how you speak to parents,

✝ how you respond to enemies.

He calls you to truth, respect, and forgiveness.

3) Your goals

Jesus is Lord over:

✝ your future,

✝ your plans,

✝ your identity.

It doesn't mean you can't want good things.

It means you don't worship good things.

4) Your words

Jesus is Lord over your mouth.

That means:

- ✝ no cruel jokes that tear down,
- ✝ no lying to save face,
- ✝ no gossip for entertainment.

Lordship shows up in daily speech.

The biggest obstacle: "But I want control"

Most sin is really a control problem.

You want to be the boss.

So following Jesus often feels like losing control.

But here's what you gain:

You gain a better King.

A King who:

- ✝ died for you,
- ✝ rose for you,
- ✝ leads with wisdom,
- ✝ and never abuses power.

Jesus is not like human leaders who use people.

He loves His people.

A clear invitation: repentance and faith

Acts 2 shows people hearing the truth about Jesus and asking what to do.

Peter tells them to repent.

Repentance is not just saying sorry.

It's turning from being your own lord and turning to Jesus as Lord.

Faith is trusting Him.

These go together:

- ✝ Turn from sin.
- ✝ Trust Jesus.
- ✝ Follow Him.

Real life: how to live under His rule this week

Try this simple daily question:

"Jesus, what does obedience look like today?"

Then choose one area to obey:

- speak kindly when you want to snap,
- tell the truth when lying feels easier,
- walk away from a temptation,
- forgive instead of replaying the hurt,
- do your school work with honesty.

Obedience is not how you earn salvation.

It's how you respond to your King.

Quick check (answer in your own words)

1. What does it mean that Jesus is Lord right now?

____

____

____

2. Why is it not enough to call Jesus "Lord" with words only?

____

____

____

3. What is one area where you resist Jesus' rule?

____

____

____

4. What is one step of obedience you can take this week?

____

____

____

Memory verse

"Then Jesus came to them and said, "All authority in heaven and on earth has been given to me." -
Matthew 28:18

Action step for the week

Do the "Lordship Check" for 6 days.

Each day, write four short lines:

1. **Jesus is Lord over my...** (choose one: mind, body, phone, words, time, friendships)
2. **Today's temptation is...** (be honest)
3. **Today's obedience is...** (one clear action)
4. **Help me, Jesus, to...** (one sentence prayer)

Keep it short. Do it before the day gets busy if you can.

Closing prayer

Lord Jesus, You are King. Forgive me for wanting control. Help me trust You and obey You. Rule my thoughts, my words, and my choices. Thank You for loving me enough to die for me. Help me live as Your follower. Amen.

PART FIVE
Welcome the Holy Spirit's Work

WEEK 24
Know the Helper:
Who the Holy Spirit Is

A lot of teens are unsure about the Holy Spirit.

Some think the Spirit is a feeling. Some think the Spirit is a force. Some think the Spirit is only about dramatic moments. Some barely think about Him at all.

But the Holy Spirit is not an "extra" for advanced Christians.

He is God.

And if you belong to Jesus, the Spirit is with you and in you. He helps you follow Christ in real life.

The big idea

The Holy Spirit is God, a real Person who lives in believers, so you can trust His help, listen to His leading through Scripture, and grow in Christ.

Key Bible passages (read these first)

- **John 14:16–17, 26** - Jesus promises the Helper who teaches.
- **John 16:7–15** - the Spirit points people to Jesus.
- **Acts 1:8** - the Spirit gives power to witness.
- **Romans 8:9–11** - the Spirit lives in believers.
- **1 Corinthians 6:19–20** - your body is a temple of the Holy Spirit.

Who the Holy Spirit is

The Holy Spirit is:

- **fully God** (not less than the Father or the Son)
- **a real Person** (not a thing)
- **the Helper Jesus promised**
- **the One who works in believers to apply God's salvation**

You can see the Spirit as a Person because Scripture shows He:

✝ teaches,

✝ speaks,

✝ guides,

✝ comforts,

✝ convicts,

✝ and can be grieved (Ephesians 4:30).

A "force" can't do those things.

What the Holy Spirit is not

Let's clear a few wrong ideas.

Not just a feeling

Feelings can change by the hour.

The Spirit is not your mood.

Sometimes you will feel close to God. Sometimes you won't. The Spirit is still real and still at work.

Not a hype moment

The Spirit can work in powerful ways, yes.

But He also works in quiet, daily ways:

✝ helping you resist temptation,

✝ giving you courage to obey,

✝ bringing Scripture to mind,

✝ pushing you to repent,

✝ growing patience in you.

Not a replacement for Scripture

Some people say, "The Spirit told me," but what they mean is, "I feel like."

The Spirit does lead, but He doesn't lead you away from God's Word. He wrote the Word. He will not contradict it.

A simple rule: **If it clashes with Scripture, it's not from the Spirit.**

What the Holy Spirit does (four clear works)

1) The Spirit points to Jesus

Jesus says the Spirit will glorify Him (John 16:14).

So the Spirit's work is not mainly to make you obsessed with yourself.

He helps you see Jesus clearly and love Him more.

A good question to ask: "Is this pulling me closer to Jesus or away from Him?"

2) The Spirit gives new life

Romans 8 says the Spirit lives in believers.

When you trust Christ, the Spirit makes you new on the inside. He takes a dead heart and gives life.

That's why Christianity is not only behavior change.

It's heart change.

3) The Spirit teaches and reminds

John 14 says the Spirit teaches and brings Jesus' words to mind.

That doesn't mean you suddenly know everything.

It means the Spirit helps you understand Scripture and apply it.

This is why daily Bible reading matters. The Spirit uses the Word like a tool.

4) The Spirit gives power to obey and speak

Acts 1:8 says the Spirit gives power to be Jesus' witnesses.

This includes courage to speak about Christ, but also strength to live like Christ.

The Spirit in your real teen life

Here's what it can look like when the Spirit is helping you:

- You feel conviction after you lie, and you choose to confess.
- You remember a Bible verse when you're tempted, and you say no.
- You feel courage to invite someone to church even though you're nervous.
- You start caring about prayer when you used to avoid it.
- You want to forgive instead of holding a grudge forever.

Those are not random personality upgrades.

That is God at work.

A common fear: "How do I know it's the Spirit and not me?"

Great question. Here are three quick checks.

Check 1: Scripture

The Spirit's leading will match God's Word.

Check 2: Jesus-focus

The Spirit points you to Jesus, not to pride.

Check 3: Fruit

The Spirit's work produces humility, repentance, love, and obedience over time.

If a "leading" makes you proud, harsh, or reckless, be careful.

Real life: how to respond to the Spirit's work

You don't "use" the Holy Spirit.

You respond to Him.

Here are three simple responses:

1. **Ask for help**

    "Holy Spirit, help me obey Jesus today."

2. **Pay attention to conviction**

    Conviction is not the same as shame.

    - o   Shame says, "You're hopeless."
    - o   Conviction says, "Turn back to God."

3. **Obey quickly**

    Small obedience builds a strong life.

Quick check (answer in your own words)

1. Who is the Holy Spirit?

    ____

    ____

    ____

    ____

2. Name one thing the Spirit is not.

    ____

    ____

    ____

    ____

3. What is one main thing the Spirit does, according to John 16?

    ____

    ____

    ____

4. Where do you need the Spirit's help most right now?

____

____

____

____

Memory verse

"And I will ask the Father, and he will give you another advocate to help you and be with you forever—" -
John 14:16

Action step for the week

Do the "Helper Prayer" for 6 days.

Each day:

1. Read **John 14:15-27** (or just verses 16-17 and 26 if you're short on time).

2. Pray this short prayer out loud:

   "Holy Spirit, help me love Jesus today.

   Help me understand God's Word.

   Help me obey in one clear way: ."

Then fill in the blank with one real thing:

- ✝ "tell the truth"
- ✝ "turn off that temptation"
- ✝ "apologize"
- ✝ "be kind at home"
- ✝ "stop gossip"

Closing prayer

Holy Spirit, thank You for being the Helper Jesus promised. Please make Jesus bigger in my heart. Teach me through Scripture. Convict me when I sin. Give me strength to obey and courage to speak about Christ. Amen.

WEEK 25
Expect Real Change:
How the Spirit Makes You New

Some teens think Christianity is mainly "be a better person."

So they try harder, fail, feel guilty, then either hide or quit.

But the gospel offers more than a fresh start on behavior.

God promises a new heart.

That new heart is not something you build by willpower.

It is something God gives by His Spirit.

This is why change is possible, even if you've been stuck for a long time.

The big idea

The Holy Spirit gives new life and a new heart, so you can become a new person in Christ and grow in real obedience.

Key Bible passages (read these first)

- **Ezekiel 36:26-27** - God gives a new heart and puts His Spirit within His people.

- **John 3:3-8** - you must be born again by the Spirit.

- **2 Corinthians 5:17** - anyone in Christ is a new creation.

- **Titus 3:4-7** - saved by God's mercy through renewal by the Holy Spirit.

What "born again" really means

Jesus tells Nicodemus, "You must be born again" (John 3).

That doesn't mean:

- you become a different human,

- you erase your personality,

- you get perfect overnight.

It means God gives you new spiritual life.

Before, you might have had religion, morals, or church habits.

But being "born again" means:

- ✝ your heart is made alive to God,
- ✝ you begin to love Christ,
- ✝ and you start to want what God wants.

It's like going from a dead phone to a charged phone.

The phone is the same phone, but now it has life and power.

The new heart promise

Ezekiel 36 is one of the clearest promises in the Bible about change.

God says He will:

- ✝ remove the heart of stone,
- ✝ give a heart of flesh,
- ✝ put His Spirit within His people,
- ✝ and cause them to walk in His ways.

Notice who does the work: God.

You respond with repentance and faith, but God is the One who changes you on the inside.

That's why Christianity is not self-fixing. It's God rescuing.

What changes first: your desires

The Spirit's work is not mainly "try harder."

It's "want differently."

The Spirit begins changing what you love.

So over time you may notice:

- ✝ you hate sin more than you used to,
- ✝ you feel convicted faster,
- ✝ you want to pray instead of run,
- ✝ you care about truth,
- ✝ you want to obey even when it's hard.

That's real change.

Not perfect. But real.

New identity before new habits

2 Corinthians 5:17 says if anyone is in Christ, he is a new creation.

So your identity is not:

- "the kid who can't change,"
- "the girl who always messes up,"
- "the boy who's addicted,"
- "the one who's too far gone."

If you are in Christ, your identity is:

- forgiven,
- alive to God,
- loved,
- being changed.

That doesn't erase consequences. It does erase hopelessness.

A common confusion: "If I'm new, why do I still struggle?"

Because new life begins, then growth continues.

Think of a newborn baby.

A baby is fully alive, but still weak. Still learning. Still growing.

In the same way, new Christians are truly alive to God, but still fighting old habits and temptations.

The presence of struggle does not prove you are fake.

It may prove you are alive.

Dead people don't fight. Living people do.

What the Spirit uses to change you

The Spirit changes you, but He doesn't usually do it by magic feelings.

He uses means, real tools God gives.

Here are three big ones:

1) God's Word

The Spirit uses Scripture to renew your mind and shape your desires.

2) Prayer

Prayer is not a performance. It's asking for help.

3) God's people

You were not meant to grow alone. Community helps you stay steady.

Real life: what "new life" looks like for a teen

Here are four signs of Spirit-given change you might see:

1. **Honesty instead of hiding**

    You confess sin sooner.

2. **Conviction instead of excuses**

    You stop blaming others for everything.

3. **New boundaries**

    You start cutting off what feeds sin.

4. **New compassion**

    You care about others more than your image.

Again: not perfect, but real.

Quick check (answer in your own words)

1. What does it mean to be "born again"?

    ____

    ____

    ____

    ____

2. What does Ezekiel 36 promise God will do in His people?

    ____

    ____

    ____

    ____

3. Why can you still struggle even after you are made new?

    ____

    ____

    ____

    ____

4. What is one sign of real change you want to see in your life?

    ____

    ____

    ____

    ____

Memory verse

"I will give you a new heart and put a new spirit in you; I will remove from you your heart of stone and give you a heart of flesh." - Ezekiel 36:26

Action step for the week

Do the "New Heart Plan" for 6 days.

Each day:

1. Read one passage:
   - Day 1: Ezekiel 36:25-27
   - Day 2: John 3:1-8
   - Day 3: Titus 3:3-7
   - Day 4: 2 Corinthians 5:14-21
   - Day 5: Romans 12:1-2
   - Day 6: Psalm 51:10-12

2. Write three short lines:
   - **Old me tends to...** (name one old pattern)

     ____

   - **God promises to...** (from the passage)

     ____

   - **Today I will...** (one small obedience step)

     ____

   Example:
   - Old me tends to hide.
   - God promises to give a new heart.
   - Today I will confess and ask for help.

Closing prayer

God, thank You for giving new life through Your Spirit. Please change my heart, not just my habits. Help me want what You want. Help me obey with joy. When I struggle, help me keep turning back to You. Amen.

WEEK 26
Fight Sin with Help:
How the Spirit Strengthens You

You can know the right thing and still do the wrong thing.

You can love Jesus and still feel pulled toward sin.

That doesn't mean you're fake. It means you're in a fight.

The Christian life is not you trying to be strong alone.

God gives you help.

The Holy Spirit strengthens you to say no to sin and yes to God, one choice at a time.

The big idea

The Holy Spirit strengthens believers to fight sin, so you can resist temptation, confess quickly, and grow in obedience.

Key Bible passages (read these first)

 † **Romans 8:12–14** - by the Spirit you put sin to death.

 † **Galatians 5:16–17** - walk by the Spirit and you won't gratify the flesh.

 † **1 Corinthians 10:13** - God provides a way of escape in temptation.

 † **Ephesians 6:10–18** - be strong in the Lord; use God's armor.

First: the fight is real

Galatians 5 says there is a conflict inside believers.

The flesh (your old sinful desires) pulls one way.

The Spirit pulls the other way.

So don't be shocked that temptation shows up.

Be ready for it.

A hard truth:

You don't drift into holiness.

You drift into sin.

Holiness takes active dependence on God.

What "fight sin" really means

Romans 8 says, "If by the Spirit you put to death the deeds of the body, you will live."

That phrase "put to death" is strong.

It means you don't pet sin.

You don't keep it as a secret friend.

You don't negotiate with it.

You cut it off.

But notice: it says **by the Spirit.**

So this is not "white-knuckle trying."

It's Spirit-powered fighting.

How the Spirit strengthens you (three main ways)

1) The Spirit gives conviction

Conviction is God's mercy.

It's the Spirit saying, "That's sin. Turn back."

Conviction is different from shame.

✝ Shame says, "You're disgusting. Hide."

✝ Conviction says, "You did wrong. Come back."

If you feel conviction, that can be a sign of life, not proof you're hopeless.

2) The Spirit brings truth to your mind

The Spirit uses Scripture to remind you of what's true.

Sometimes it's a verse you memorized. Sometimes it's a truth you learned. Sometimes it's a warning that hits your conscience.

This is why Week 6 mattered: daily Scripture fills your mind with weapons for the fight.

3) The Spirit gives power to obey

The Spirit doesn't only show you what is right.

He helps you do it.

He strengthens your will. He helps you take the next right step.

Even if you feel weak, you can ask for strength and obey.

A simple picture: temptation is a doorway

1 Corinthians 10:13 says temptation is common, and God provides a way of escape.

That doesn't always mean temptation disappears.

It often means God gives you a door to walk through.

The "escape" might be:

- turning off your phone,
- leaving the room,
- texting a trusted friend,
- telling the truth,
- going for a walk,
- opening your Bible,
- asking for prayer.

But you have to take the door.

The "three moves" of Spirit-led fighting

Here's a simple plan you can use in the moment.

Move 1: Name the temptation

Don't call it "a vibe" or "a bad habit."

Name it:

- lust
- anger
- envy
- lying
- pride
- gossip
- bitterness

Naming it helps you face it.

Move 2: Cut off the fuel

Sin grows when it gets fed.

So ask:

"What is feeding this?"

Then cut it off as quickly as you can:

+ unfollow,

+ delete,

+ block,

+ step away,

+ change your routine,

+ stop being alone with the temptation.

This is not legalism. This is wisdom.

Jesus said to cut off what causes you to sin (Matthew 5:29–30). He was not telling you to harm your body. He was telling you to take sin seriously.

Move 3: Replace with obedience

Don't only say "no."

Say "yes" to something better:

+ pray,

+ read a short passage,

+ do a good task,

+ speak kindly,

+ confess to someone safe,

+ serve someone.

Sin hates replacement. It thrives in empty space.

The armor of God: don't fight naked

Ephesians 6 shows the Christian life is spiritual war.

God gives armor:

+ truth

+ righteousness

+ gospel peace

+ faith

+ salvation

+ the Word of God

+ prayer

This doesn't mean you're scared of demons all day.

It means you take the fight seriously, and you use God's tools.

Real life: how this hits teen temptations

Let's get specific.

When temptation is on your phone

The phone is not neutral. It trains you.

Spirit-led fighting might look like:

- moving your phone out of your room at night,
- putting limits on apps,
- turning off private browsing,
- not staying alone when you're weak,
- asking a trusted adult for accountability.

When temptation is anger

Anger can feel powerful.

But Spirit-led fighting might look like:

- stopping before you text back,
- waiting 10 minutes,
- speaking calmly,
- forgiving,
- asking God for self-control.

When temptation is people-pleasing

This one is sneaky.

Spirit-led fighting might look like:

- saying no to gossip,
- not joining in when someone is mocked,
- obeying God even when friends roll their eyes.

Quick check (answer in your own words)

1. What does Romans 8 say about fighting sin?

   ____

   ____

   ____

   ____

2. What is the difference between conviction and shame?

   ____

   ____

   ____

3. What is one "fuel" that feeds your strongest temptation?

____

____

____

4. What is one "way of escape" you can take next time?

____

____

____

Memory verse

"Walk by the Spirit, and you will not gratify the desires of the flesh." — Galatians 5:16

Action step for the week

Create a "Fight Plan" for one repeated sin.

1. Write the sin clearly.
2. Write three triggers (what usually comes before it).
3. Write one escape door for each trigger.
4. Write one replacement action for each escape door.
5. Pray for help every day.

Example:

✝ Sin: gossip

✝ Trigger: group chat drama

✝ Escape: mute the chat and leave it for 24 hours

✝ Replace: text one encouraging thing to someone instead

Do this plan for 7 days.

Closing prayer

Holy Spirit, I need Your help. Please show me my sin clearly and give me strength to turn away. Help me take the escape door when temptation comes. Fill my mind with Your truth. Make me steady and clean in my choices. Amen.

WEEK 27
Grow Real Fruit:
What God Changes Over Time

Some teens want change fast.

You pray once and hope the struggle disappears. You read one chapter and hope your attitude becomes perfect.

But growth usually works like a tree, not like a light switch.

Trees don't grow overnight.

They grow slowly, steadily, and quietly, if their roots stay fed.

The Bible calls this kind of growth **fruit**.

Fruit is the outward result of inward life.

If the Holy Spirit lives in you, God will grow real fruit over time.

The big idea

The Holy Spirit grows Christlike fruit in believers over time, so you can keep walking with God, not quitting when growth feels slow.

Key Bible passages (read these first)

✝ **Galatians 5:22–23** - the fruit of the Spirit.

✝ **John 15:1–11** - abide in Christ and bear fruit.

✝ **Philippians 1:6** - God will finish what He started.

✝ **Colossians 1:9–10** - growing in fruit comes through knowing God's will.

What "fruit of the Spirit" means

Galatians 5 lists the fruit:

✝ love	✝ patience	✝ faithfulness
✝ joy	✝ kindness	✝ gentleness
✝ peace	✝ goodness	✝ self-control

Notice it says "fruit," not "fruits," like a bunch of different trees.

It's one kind of life, Christlike life, showing up in different ways.

Also notice it does not say: "Fruit of your personality."

It says "fruit of the Spirit."

That means this growth is not mainly you trying to become a nicer person.

It's God changing you from the inside.

Fruit is not the same as gifts

Some teens confuse gifts with fruit.

A person can be talented and still be unkind.

A person can be bold and still be proud.

Spiritual gifts are abilities God gives to serve others.

Fruit is character God grows to make you more like Jesus.

God cares about both.

But fruit matters more than looking impressive.

"Abide" means stay close

John 15 is Jesus' picture of growth.

He says He is the vine and we are the branches.

Branches don't produce fruit by trying really hard.

They produce fruit by staying connected.

That's what "abide" means:

 stay close, stay connected, keep trusting, keep listening.

How do you abide?

- ✝ stay in God's Word,
- ✝ stay in prayer,
- ✝ stay in fellowship with believers,
- ✝ keep turning from sin,
- ✝ keep returning to Christ.

Why growth feels slow

Growth often feels slow for three reasons:

1) You notice your sin more

As you grow, your conscience gets sharper.

That can feel like you're getting worse.

Sometimes you're not getting worse. You're seeing more clearly.

2) God is changing deeper roots

God often works below the surface first.

He may be changing pride, fear, control, and self-centeredness.

Those roots take time.

3) You want instant results

Culture trains you for quick results.

God often trains you for lasting results.

Lasting growth takes time.

How to tell if you're growing (even if you still struggle)

Here are signs of real fruit:

- You repent faster than you used to.
- You hate sin more than you used to.
- You forgive more than you used to.
- You're more honest than you used to.
- You're more willing to obey than you used to.
- You care less about looking cool and more about being faithful.

You might still fight sin, but the direction is changing.

The fruit list in real teen language

Let's put the fruit into everyday examples.

- **Love:** you choose what's best for others, not just what's easy.
- **Joy:** you have a steady gladness even on rough days.
- **Peace:** you don't panic as fast; you trust God more.
- **Patience:** you don't blow up as quickly when annoyed.
- **Kindness:** you treat people with respect, even when they can't help you.
- **Goodness:** you do what is right when no one is watching.
- **Faithfulness:** you keep your word and show up.
- **Gentleness:** you speak truth without cruelty.
- **Self-control:** you say no to sin, even when you feel pulled.

Fruit doesn't mean you never fail.

It means your life begins to look more like Jesus.

Real life: how to cooperate with God's growth

You can't grow fruit by force.

But you can help your "roots" stay healthy.

Here are four simple practices:

1) Stay in Scripture

Even short daily reading matters.

Roots need water.

2) Pray honestly

Not long prayers. Real prayers.

"God, help me be patient with my family today."

3) Confess quickly

Hidden sin kills growth.

Confession brings sin into the light.

4) Choose steady community

You grow better with other believers.

Isolation feeds sin.

Quick check (answer in your own words)

1. What is the fruit of the Spirit?

    ____

    ____

    ____

    ____

2. What does it mean to "abide" in Christ?

    ____

    ____

    ____

    ____

3. What fruit do you want God to grow most in you right now?

    ____

    ____

    ____

    ____

4. What is one habit that helps your roots stay healthy?

____

____

____

____

Memory verse

"But the fruit of the Spirit is love, joy, peace, forbearance, kindness, goodness, faithfulness," - Galatians 5:22

Action step for the week

Do the "Fruit Tracker" for 7 days.

1. Pick **one** fruit to focus on (like patience or self-control).

2. Each day, write:

      o Today I needed this fruit when...

    ____

      o I responded by...

    ____

      o Next time, with God's help, I will...

    ____

3. Pray one sentence:

    "Holy Spirit, grow _______________________ in me today."

Keep it short. The point is steady attention, not perfect performance.

Closing prayer

Holy Spirit, please grow real fruit in me. Help me stay close to Jesus. Help me not quit when growth feels slow. Make my character look more like Christ, for Your glory and for the good of others. Amen.

PART SIX
Receive Salvation God's Way

WEEK 28
Get the Gospel Clear:
The Good News in One Sentence

If someone asked you, "What is the gospel?" could you answer without freezing?

A lot of teens can say, "Jesus died for me," and that's true. But sometimes the meaning is fuzzy.

The gospel is not:

- ✝ "Be a good person."
- ✝ "Go to church."
- ✝ "God helps those who help themselves."
- ✝ "Try harder."

The gospel is good news because it tells you what God has done for sinners in Jesus.

This week is about clarity.

Not so you can sound smart.

So you can live with steady hope and share it with confidence.

The big idea

The gospel is the good news that God saves sinners through Jesus' life, death, and resurrection, so you can be forgiven, made new, and live under Christ's rule.

Key Bible passages (read these first)

- ✝ **1 Corinthians 15:1–4** - the gospel: Christ died, was buried, and rose.
- ✝ **Romans 1:16–17** - the gospel is God's power to save.
- ✝ **Romans 3:23–24** - all sin; we are justified by grace.
- ✝ **Mark 1:14–15** - repent and believe the gospel.

The gospel in one sentence

Here's a clear one-sentence gospel:

The gospel is the good news that God saves sinners by grace through faith in Jesus Christ, who died for our sins and rose again, so we can be forgiven and live with Him as our King.

That's a full sentence, but it's still one sentence.

Now let's break it down so it sticks.

The gospel has four parts you must keep together

If you drop one part, the message gets twisted.

1) God

The gospel starts with God, not you.

God is holy, good, and just.

That means sin matters, and rescue is needed.

2) Us

We are sinners.

Not just "imperfect." Guilty.

We fall short of God's glory.

We can't fix ourselves.

3) Jesus

Jesus is the Savior God promised.

He lived without sin.

He died in our place.

He rose from the dead.

He is Lord.

4) Response

The gospel calls for a response: **repent and believe** (Mark 1:15).

Repentance is turning from sin and self-rule.

Faith is trusting Jesus, not your own goodness.

A simple memory tool: "G-O-S-P-E-L"

This can help you explain it fast:

✝ **G** - God is holy and good.

✝ **O** - Our sin separates us.

✝ **S** - Salvation is in Jesus alone.

✝ **P** - Payment was made at the cross.

✝ **E** - Everyone must respond with repentance and faith.

✝ **L** - Life with Jesus begins now and lasts forever.

You don't have to use this every time, but it helps.

What the gospel is not

This matters because fake gospels are everywhere.

Not self-help

The gospel is not tips to improve your life.

It's news about what God did to save you.

Not moral improvement

Good works matter, but they come after salvation, not before it.

Not "God loves you, so nothing matters"

God's love is holy love.

It forgives sin, but it also calls you out of sin.

Not "Jesus plus"

Not Jesus plus your performance.

Not Jesus plus your church attendance.

Not Jesus plus your pain.

Jesus alone saves.

Why teens need gospel clarity

Because you'll face pressure.

Pressure to prove yourself. Pressure to fit in. Pressure to pretend you're fine. Pressure to believe lies about God.

The gospel gives you a steady center:

✝ You're more sinful than you like to admit.

✝ You're more loved in Christ than you can earn.

That combination keeps you humble and hopeful.

Real life: what happens when you forget the gospel

When you forget the gospel, you slide into one of two ditches.

Ditch 1: Pride

You think you're doing "better" than others, so you look down.

Ditch 2: Despair

You mess up and think God is done with you.

The gospel keeps you out of both.

It says: You're saved by grace, so you can't boast. You're saved by grace, so you don't have to panic.

Quick check (answer in your own words)

1. Write the gospel in one sentence (your own words).

    ____

    ____

    ____

    ____

2. What are the four parts of the gospel message?

    ____

    ____

    ____

    ____

3. What is one fake gospel you hear a lot?

    ____

    ____

    ____

    ____

4. Which ditch do you fall into more: pride or despair? Why?

    ____

    ____

    ____

    ____

Memory verse

> *"For what I received I passed on to you as of first
> importance: that Christ died for our sins according to the
> Scriptures, that he was buried, that he was raised on the
> third day according to the Scriptures," -*
> *1 Corinthians 15:3–4*

Action step for the week

Practice your one-sentence gospel out loud for 5 days.

Here's how:

1. Write your one sentence on a card or in your notes app.

2. Say it out loud once a day.

3. Each day, add one short follow-up sentence that explains one part:
    o   Day 1: God's holiness
    o   Day 2: our sin
    o   Day 3: Jesus' cross
    o   Day 4: resurrection
    o   Day 5: repent and believe

Then pray for one friend who needs the gospel.

You don't have to force a conversation.

Just ask God to give you an open door.

Closing prayer

God, thank You for the good news. Help me understand the gospel clearly and believe it deeply. Keep me from pride and despair. Help me trust Jesus, love Him, and share this good news with courage and kindness. Amen.

WEEK 29
Repent for Real:
What Turning Back to God Means

A lot of people think repentance means "feeling bad."

Some think it means saying sorry, then doing the same thing tomorrow.

Others think repentance is only for "big sins."

The Bible means something clearer.

Repentance is a change of direction.

It's turning from sin and turning to God. Not to earn love, but because God is better than the sin that's killing you.

The big idea

Repentance is turning from sin to God with honesty and obedience, so you can walk in forgiveness and real change through Jesus.

Key Bible passages (read these first)

- ✝ **Mark 1:14–15** - Jesus calls people to repent and believe.
- ✝ **Acts 2:37–39** - repent and receive forgiveness.
- ✝ **2 Corinthians 7:9–10** - worldly sorrow vs. godly sorrow.
- ✝ **1 John 1:8–10** - confess sin and receive cleansing.
- ✝ **Luke 15:11–24** - the prodigal son comes home.

What repentance is (simple and clear)

Repentance includes three parts that belong together:

1. **Mind:** you agree with God about your sin.
2. **Heart:** you hate what is wrong and want what is right.
3. **Life:** you turn and obey in a real way.

Repentance is not perfection.

Repentance is a real turn.

What repentance is not

This helps you avoid fake repentance.

Not just getting caught

If you only "repent" because you got caught, that's fear, not repentance.

Fear might stop you for a moment. It won't change your heart.

Not just feelings

You can cry and still cling to sin.

Tears can be real, but tears alone are not repentance.

Not paying God back

You can't repay Jesus.

Repentance is not you trying to earn forgiveness.

It's you returning to the One who forgives.

The difference between worldly sorrow and godly sorrow

2 Corinthians 7 is one of the clearest places in the Bible on this.

Worldly sorrow often sounds like:

- ✝ "I hate the consequences."
- ✝ "I hate that people know."
- ✝ "I hate that I look bad."
- ✝ "I hate that I feel guilty."

It can lead to more hiding, more anger, or more hopelessness.

Godly sorrow sounds like:

- ✝ "God, I sinned against You."
- ✝ "This is wrong, and I don't want it."
- ✝ "I want to change."
- ✝ "Help me obey."

Godly sorrow leads to repentance.

A picture that makes it stick: the prodigal son

Luke 15 shows a son who runs from his father, wastes his life, and ends up empty.

Then something changes.

He "comes to himself."

He decides to return, confess, and ask for mercy.

He doesn't show up with excuses. He shows up with honesty.

And the father runs to him.

That story does not say sin is fine.

It says God welcomes repentant sinners.

Why repentance is good news

Repentance can sound heavy until you see what it gives you.

Repentance gives you:

- ✝ a clean start instead of a double life,
- ✝ peace instead of constant hiding,
- ✝ freedom instead of chains,
- ✝ closeness with God instead of distance.

Repentance is painful for a moment, but it heals.

Repentance and faith go together

Jesus says, "Repent and believe the gospel" (Mark 1:15).

Repentance is turning from sin.

Faith is turning to Jesus.

If you only repent without faith, you end up trying to fix yourself.

If you claim faith without repentance, you end up using Jesus as a cover for sin.

Real conversion includes both.

Real life: what real repentance looks like for teens

Here are three teen-level examples.

1) Gossip

Fake repentance: "Sorry if you got hurt."

Real repentance: "I talked about you. That was wrong. Will you forgive me?" Then you stop feeding the drama.

2) Porn or sexual sin

Fake repentance: "I feel gross," then you keep private access and late-night scrolling.

Real repentance: you confess to God, tell a trusted adult, cut off sources, and set new boundaries.

3) Anger

Fake repentance: "That's just how I am."

Real repentance: you confess, apologize, and start practicing self-control steps before you blow up.

Repentance always includes a turn.

A simple repentance plan you can use anytime (the "5R" plan)

When you sin, do this:

1. **Realize** - "This is sin."
2. **Responsibility** - "I chose this."
3. **Request** - "God, forgive me because of Jesus."
4. **Remove** - cut off what feeds it (app, chat, secret routine).
5. **Replace** - obey in one clear way (truth, apology, service, prayer).

Keep it simple. Do it fast. Don't wait a week.

Quick check (answer in your own words)

1. What is repentance?

____

____

____

____

2. What is one sign of fake repentance?

____

____

____

____

3. What is the difference between worldly sorrow and godly sorrow?

____

____

____

____

4. What is one sin you need to repent of in a real way this week?

____

____

____

Memory verse

"The time has come," he said. "The kingdom of God has come near. Repent and believe the good news!" -
Mark 1:15

Action step for the week

Do one "real repentance" step within 48 hours.

1. Read **1 John 1:8–10**.

2. Write one honest sentence:

    "God, I sinned by _________________________________."

3. Then do one real "turn" action:

    o   confess to a trusted parent/pastor/leader,

    o   apologize to someone you hurt,

    o   delete or block what feeds temptation,

    o   leave a chat that pulls you into sin,

    o   make a plan to avoid the trigger.

If your sin is ongoing and heavy, don't stay alone. Bring it into the light with a safe, mature believer.

Closing prayer

God, I admit my sin. I don't want to hide. Please forgive me through Jesus. Help me turn away from what is wrong. Give me strength to obey You today. Thank You for welcoming repentant sinners. Amen.

WEEK 30
Trust Jesus:
What Faith Is (and What It Isn't)

A lot of teens say, "Yeah, I believe in God."

But faith in the Bible is more than agreeing God exists.

You can believe facts about Jesus and still not trust Him.

Real faith is not a vibe. It's not pretending you never doubt. It's not trying to earn points with God.

Faith is trusting Jesus like He's real, like He's Lord, and like you need Him.

The big idea

Saving faith is trusting Jesus Himself, who He is and what He has done, so you rely on Him, follow Him, and stop trusting yourself.

Key Bible passages (read these first)

- ✝ **Ephesians 2:8–9** - saved by grace through faith, not works.
- ✝ **Romans 10:9–13** - believe and confess Jesus as Lord.
- ✝ **James 2:17–20** - facts without trust and obedience are dead.
- ✝ **John 20:30–31** - believe in Jesus and have life in His name.
- ✝ **Mark 9:24** - "I believe; help my unbelief!"

What faith is

Faith is not mainly a feeling.

Faith is **relying.**

Here's a clear way to say it:

Faith is trusting Jesus to save you and lead you.

That includes three parts:

1) Knowing the truth

You can't trust someone you don't know.

Faith starts with truth about Jesus:

- ✝ He is God the Son,
- ✝ He became man,
- ✝ He lived without sin,
- ✝ He died for sinners,
- ✝ He rose again,
- ✝ He is Lord.

2) Agreeing the truth is true

Not "maybe." Not "probably."

You agree: God's message is true.

3) Trusting Jesus personally

This is the part many miss.

You stop leaning on yourself and lean on Christ.

It's like stepping onto a bridge.

You can study the bridge, talk about the bridge, even say "I believe bridges exist."

But you only trust the bridge when you put your weight on it.

What faith is not

Let's name the common confusion.

Faith is not "being a good person"

Ephesians 2 says you are saved by grace through faith, not by works.

Good works matter, but they don't save.

If your "faith" is mostly, "I'm nicer than some people," that's not saving faith.

Faith is not "church stuff"

Going to church is good.

But church attendance is not the same as trusting Jesus.

You can sit in a garage and still not be a car.

Faith is not "never doubting"

Mark 9:24 is honest: "I believe; help my unbelief!"

That's real faith talking.

Faith can exist with questions.

The difference is: faith brings questions to Jesus instead of running away from Him.

Faith is not "I said a prayer once"

A prayer can be real.

But faith is not a one-time magic sentence.

Faith is a real trust that shows up over time.

James 2: a hard passage made simple

James says faith without works is dead.

He's not saying you earn salvation by works.

He's saying real faith is not just words. Real faith produces a changed life.

If someone claims to trust Jesus but has zero desire to obey Him, something is off.

Not perfect obedience.

Real direction.

How to tell if you're trusting Jesus

Ask yourself these questions:

- Do I believe I need Jesus, or do I think I'm fine?
- Do I talk to Jesus honestly, or do I avoid Him when I sin?
- Do I want to obey Him, even when I struggle?
- When I fail, do I return to Him or hide?

These questions don't save you.

They help you see if your faith is real.

Real life: how faith works on a normal day

Faith is not only for big moments like camp or church.

Faith is for:

- saying no to temptation when no one is watching,
- telling the truth when lying would be easier,
- asking God for help before you panic,
- forgiving when you want revenge,
- obeying even when friends laugh.

Faith looks like trust plus action.

Not action to earn love.

Action because you trust Jesus.

A simple sentence you can pray

If you're unsure where you stand, you can pray this honestly:

"Jesus, I trust You. Help me trust You more."

That's not fake. That's a real prayer.

Quick check (answer in your own words)

1. What are the three parts of faith (know, agree, trust)?

   ____

   ____

   ____

   ____

2. Which false version of faith do you fall into most: "being good," "church stuff," or "no doubt allowed"?

   ____

   ____

   ____

   ____

3. Why does James say faith without works is dead?

   ____

   ____

   ____

   ____

4. What is one area where you need to trust Jesus this week?

   ____

   ____

   ____

   ____

Memory verse

> *"For it is by grace you have been saved, through faith—
> and this is not from yourselves, it is the gift of God— not
> by works, so that no one can boast." - Ephesians 2:8–9*

Action step for the week

Do the "Weight on Jesus" practice for 6 days.

Each day:

1. Read one passage:
    - o Day 1: John 20:30–31
    - o Day 2: Romans 10:9–13
    - o Day 3: Ephesians 2:1–10
    - o Day 4: Mark 9:14–29
    - o Day 5: James 2:14–18
    - o Day 6: Psalm 56:3–4

2. Write two lines:
    - o **Today I'm tempted to trust...** (myself, friends, control, comfort, approval)

    ____

    ____

    ____

    ____

    - o **Today I will trust Jesus by...** (one clear action)

    ____

    ____

    ____

    ____

Example: "Today I'm tempted to trust approval. Today I will trust Jesus by telling the truth even if it's awkward."

Closing prayer

Lord Jesus, I don't want faith to be only words. Help me trust You for forgiveness and for daily strength. When I doubt, help me come to You. Teach me to obey You because You are good and You are Lord. Amen.

WEEK 31
Stand on Grace:
Saved by God, Not Good Behavior

A lot of teens live like God has a points system.

Good day: God likes me. Bad day: God is done with me.

That way of living will crush you.

It will also make you fake, because you'll start hiding your mess to look "spiritual."

The Bible gives a better foundation:

You are saved by God's grace, not by your good behavior.

Grace means God gives what you don't deserve.

That's why the gospel is good news.

The big idea

You are saved by grace, so you can stop trying to earn God's love, rest in Christ's finished work, and obey from gratitude.

Key Bible passages (read these first)

- **Ephesians 2:8–10** - saved by grace through faith, created for good works.

- **Titus 3:4–7** - saved by mercy, not our works.

- **Romans 11:6** - grace and works don't mix as the basis of salvation.

- **Luke 18:9–14** - the tax collector is made right, not the self-trusting Pharisee.

What grace is

Grace is God's kindness to people who don't deserve it.

It includes:

- **forgiveness** (your guilt is removed in Christ)

- **acceptance** (God welcomes you in Christ)

- **help** (God gives strength to obey)

Grace is not God pretending sin is fine.

Grace is God paying for sin through Jesus, then giving mercy to sinners.

What grace is not

Let's clear the confusion.

Grace is not "God helps those who help themselves"

That line is popular, but it's not the gospel.

The gospel says God helps people who **can't** save themselves.

Grace is not a license to sin

Some people treat grace like a free pass.

"If God forgives, then I can do whatever."

That's not grace. That's using God.

Real grace changes your heart so you want to obey.

Grace is not "God loves me because I'm doing well"

If that were true, God's love would rise and fall with your behavior.

But Scripture says you're saved by grace, not by works.

So your performance is not the foundation.

Jesus is.

Why grace matters so much for teens

Because teen life is full of pressure.

Pressure to:

✝ look good,

✝ fit in,

✝ be impressive,

✝ get approval,

✝ avoid shame.

If you bring that pressure into your relationship with God, you'll treat Him like another judge.

Grace says God is not waiting for you to earn your way in.

In Christ, He already brought you in.

Two common traps grace saves you from

Trap 1: Pride

If you think you're accepted because you're doing well, you'll look down on others.

Grace kills pride.

You can't brag about a gift you didn't earn.

Trap 2: Despair

If you think you're accepted because you're doing well, then one failure can make you spiral.

Grace kills despair.

You can repent, return, and keep going.

The right order: grace first, then growth

Ephesians 2:8–10 shows the order clearly.

1. **Saved by grace through faith** (not works).
2. **Created for good works** (God prepared them).

So good works matter, but they are the result, not the price.

A helpful sentence: **You don't work for salvation. You work from salvation.**

Real life: what grace changes this week

Grace changes how you handle three big moments:

1) When you fail

Instead of hiding, you confess.

Instead of quitting, you return.

You say, "Jesus paid for this. I'm coming back."

2) When you obey

You don't obey to impress God.

You obey because you trust Him and love Him.

That makes obedience lighter, not lazy.

3) When you see someone else mess up

Grace makes you humble and helpful.

You can correct sin without acting superior.

Quick check (answer in your own words)

1. What is grace?

    ____

    ____

    ____

2. Why can't salvation be based on both grace and works at the same
    time?

    ____

    ____

    ____

3. Which trap do you fall into more: pride or despair?

    ____

    ____

    ____

4. How should grace change the way you respond after you sin?

    ____

    ____

    ____

Memory verse

> *"he saved us, not because of righteous things we had done,
> but because of his mercy. He saved us through the
> washing of rebirth and renewal by the Holy Spirit," -*
> *Titus 3:5*

Action step for the week

Do the "Grace vs. Points" practice for 6 days.

Each day, write two short lines:

1. **Points thinking says:** (write a lie you're tempted to believe)

    Examples: "God is mad at me," "I have to earn it," "I'm better
    than them."

2. **Grace says:** (write a truth from Scripture)

Examples: "Jesus paid for my sin," "God welcomes repentant sinners," "I'm saved by mercy."

Then do one small obedience step as a thank-you to God:

- ✝ apologize,
- ✝ tell the truth,
- ✝ serve someone,
- ✝ shut down temptation,
- ✝ pray for a friend.

Closing prayer

God, thank You for grace. Forgive me for trying to earn what Jesus already paid for. Help me rest in Christ. Help me obey You because I love You, not because I'm trying to win Your love. Amen.

WEEK 32
Know You're Accepted: Justification Made Simple

Some teens think God accepts them like a teacher accepts late work.

"You're on thin ice, but I'll allow it."

So they live nervous.

They think one bad week could cancel them.

Justification is the Bible's answer to that fear.

Justification is a courtroom word. It tells you how God treats you when you trust Jesus.

The big idea

Justification means God declares sinners righteous in Christ, so you can know you're accepted, stop trying to earn approval, and live with peace.

Key Bible passages (read these first)

- ✝ **Romans 3:21–26** - God is just and makes sinners right through Jesus.
- ✝ **Romans 5:1** - justified by faith, we have peace with God.
- ✝ **Luke 18:9–14** - the humble sinner is made right with God.
- ✝ **Philippians 3:8–9** - not my righteousness, but Christ's.

What justification is (plain and clear)

Justification is God's legal declaration that you are righteous because of Jesus.

That means:

- ✝ God is the Judge.
- ✝ You are guilty on your own.
- ✝ Jesus paid for your sin.

✝ Jesus gives you His righteousness.

✝ God declares you "right" with Him when you trust Christ.

This is not God ignoring sin.

It's God dealing with sin through the cross, then welcoming you as clean in His sight.

Justification is not the same as "being changed"

This part matters.

Justification is about your **status** with God.

It answers: "Am I accepted?"

Sanctification (Week 33) is about your **growth**.

It answers: "Am I becoming more like Jesus?"

So:

✝ Justification happens once.

✝ Growth happens over time.

You don't get accepted more as you grow.

You grow because you're accepted.

How God can declare you righteous and still be just

Romans 3 says God is just, and He justifies the one who has faith in Jesus.

How?

Because Jesus took the punishment your sin deserved.

So God doesn't pretend you're innocent.

He treats Jesus as guilty in your place, then treats you as righteous in Christ.

This is the heart of the gospel.

A simple picture: the swap

2 Corinthians 5:21 says Jesus, who knew no sin, was made sin for us, so we could become righteous in Him.

Think of it like a swap:

✝ Your sin goes to Jesus.

✝ His righteousness comes to you.

So when God looks at you in Christ, He sees you covered in Christ's righteousness.

That's why Romans 5:1 says you have peace with God.

Not "maybe peace."

Peace.

What justification changes in your daily life

1) It changes how you handle guilt

Guilt is real when you sin.

But guilt is not meant to own you.

If you're justified, you can confess sin without panic.

You can say: "I sinned. Jesus paid for it. I'm coming back to God."

2) It changes how you handle comparison

If you think you're accepted because you're "better," you'll look down on others.

If you think you're accepted because you're "worse," you'll feel hopeless.

Justification ends both.

Your acceptance is not based on your ranking.

It's based on Jesus.

3) It changes how you handle anxiety about God

Some teens pray like God is annoyed.

Justification says God has welcomed you.

You can come close.

You can ask for help.

You can be honest.

A common question: "What if I don't feel accepted?"

Feelings matter, but they're not the judge.

God is.

Justification is based on what God declares, not what you feel at 11 p.m. on a hard day.

So when feelings shout, you return to Scripture.

Romans 5:1 is steady even when you're shaky.

Quick check (answer in your own words)

1. What does justification mean?

   ----

2. Why is justification a one-time declaration, not a slow process?

   ----

3. What is the difference between justification and sanctification?

   ----

4. What is one fear you carry that justification answers?

Memory verse

> *"Therefore, since we have been justified through faith, we have peace with God through our Lord Jesus Christ," -*
> *Romans 5:1*

Action step for the week

Do the "Peace With God" practice for 6 days.

Each day:

1. Read **Romans 5:1–5.**
2. Write two lines:

   o **Because I am justified...** (one truth)

      ----

o   **Today I will...** (one response)

____

____

Examples:

✝   "Because I am justified, I will confess quickly instead of hiding."

✝   "Because I am justified, I will pray with confidence."

✝   "Because I am justified, I will stop comparing myself to others."

Closing prayer

God, thank You that You accept me in Christ. Thank You that Jesus paid for my sin and gives me His righteousness. Help me live in peace with You. Help me stop trying to earn what You have already given. Amen.

WEEK 33
Live Set Apart: Sanctification in Real Life

Justification means God declares you right with Him in Christ (Week 32).

Sanctification is what comes next.

Sanctification means God keeps changing you so your life starts to match what He has already said is true about you.

It's not instant.

It's real.

And it shows up in normal places: your phone, your words, your friendships, your choices, and your habits.

The big idea

Sanctification is God making you more like Jesus over time, so you grow in obedience, fight sin, and live a life set apart for God.

Key Bible passages (read these first)

- ✝ **1 Thessalonians 4:3–8** - God's will is your sanctification.
- ✝ **Philippians 2:12–13** - you work it out because God works in you.
- ✝ **Romans 12:1–2** - be transformed by renewing your mind.
- ✝ **John 17:17** - God sets His people apart by His truth.
- ✝ **Galatians 5:16–25** - walk by the Spirit and grow fruit.

What sanctification is (simple and clear)

Sanctification means:

- ✝ God is changing your **desires**
- ✝ God is changing your **thinking**
- ✝ God is changing your **choices**
- ✝ God is changing your **habits**

✝ God is changing your **character**

It's becoming more like Jesus from the inside out.

This is not you trying to earn acceptance.

You're already accepted in Christ.

This is you learning to live like you belong to Him.

Who does the work?

Philippians 2 gives both sides:

✝ You are called to obey and take action.

✝ God is the One giving you the desire and strength.

So sanctification is not:

✝ "Let go and do nothing."

✝ "Try harder alone."

It's: **depend on God, then obey.**

"Set apart" doesn't mean "weird"

Being set apart doesn't mean you act strange to get attention.

It means your life has a different center.

You don't follow Jesus for a brand.

You follow Jesus because He is Lord.

So being set apart often looks like:

✝ you tell the truth when others lie,

✝ you say no when others pressure you,

✝ you forgive when others hold grudges,

✝ you stay pure when others treat bodies like toys,

✝ you stay kind when others are cruel.

Four big areas where sanctification shows up

1) Your mind

Romans 12 says you're transformed by renewing your mind.

Your mind gets shaped by what you feed it.

Ask:

✝ What am I watching?

✝ What am I listening to?

✝ What pages and accounts shape my thoughts?

✝ What lies am I believing?

God changes you by replacing lies with truth.

That's why Scripture matters every day.

2) Your body

1 Thessalonians 4 connects sanctification to purity.

God cares what you do with your body because your body belongs to Him.

This includes:

- what you look at,
- what you do in secret,
- how you treat people you're attracted to,
- what boundaries you keep.

Purity isn't about shame.

It's about honoring God and protecting your heart.

3) Your words

Sanctification shows up in your mouth fast.

- sarcasm that cuts
- gossip that spreads
- lies to protect your image
- jokes that celebrate sin

God can change your speech.

He can make you someone who builds trust, not breaks it.

4) Your relationships

Sanctification affects who you become around people.

It shows up when you:

- stop using people,
- stop needing constant approval,
- stop flirting with temptation,
- stop staying silent when someone is bullied,
- start choosing friends who push you toward Christ.

A normal pattern of growth

Most teens want a straight line: up and up and up.

Growth is often messier than that.

It looks more like:

+ progress,
+ then a fall,
+ then repentance,
+ then wiser boundaries,
+ then stronger habits,
+ then more progress.

A fall is not the end if you repent and keep walking.

The danger is not failing.

The danger is giving up and calling sin "fine."

How God uses ordinary habits to change you

Sanctification often happens through simple habits done over time:

+ reading Scripture
+ prayer
+ church and community
+ confession
+ serving others
+ taking the Lord's Supper with a serious heart (when your church practices it)

None of these earn salvation.

They are ways God feeds your faith and strengthens obedience.

Real life: a teen plan for sanctification (the "3S plan")

Use this for one struggle you want to grow in.

Step 1: Spot it

Name one sin pattern:

☐ lying

☐ anger

☐ gossip

☐ envy

☐ people-pleasing

☐ laziness

Write it clearly. ____

Step 2: Shut the door

What feeds it?

Cut off the fuel:

- delete the app
- leave the chat
- stop being alone at night with your phone
- change your route
- set limits
- ask for accountability

This is wisdom, not fear.

Step 3: Start the good

Replace sin with obedience:

- truth instead of lying
- kindness instead of cruelty
- prayer instead of panic
- serving instead of selfishness

Replacement matters because empty space invites the same sin back.

Quick check (answer in your own words)

1. What is sanctification?

   ____

   ____

   ____

   ____

2. Why is sanctification not the same as justification?

   ____

   ____

   ____

   ____

3. Where do you need growth most right now: mind, body, words, or relationships?

   ____

   ____

   ____

4. What is one "door" you need to shut this week?

____

____

____

____

Memory verse

"It is God's will that you should be sanctified: that you should avoid sexual immorality;" - 1 Thessalonians 4:3

Action step for the week

Do the "One Area Growth Plan" for 7 days.

1. Pick **one** area: mind, body, words, or relationships.
2. Each day, write three lines:
   - **Spot:** "Today I was tempted to _______________________

     ____

   - **Shut:** "So I will shut the door by _______________________

     ____

   - **Start:** "And I will obey by_______________________________

     ____

Keep it honest and small.

Example (words):

- Spot: "I wanted to gossip about her."
- Shut: "I will leave that chat for today."
- Start: "I will say one kind thing instead."

Closing prayer

God, thank You that You don't leave me the same. Please change me to be more like Jesus. Help me fight sin with Your help. Give me strength to obey in small ways today. Grow real holiness in my life. Amen.

WEEK 34
Hold On in Doubt:
Can a Christian Lose Salvation?

Some teens feel strong faith one week, then feel nothing the next.

Then the scary thought shows up:

"What if I'm not really saved?"

"What if God gives up on me?"

"What if I lose salvation because I keep messing up?"

This week is about steady hope.

The Bible gives both:

- serious warnings (don't play with sin), and
- strong comfort (God keeps His people).

So we'll hold both, like the Bible does.

The big idea

True Christians are kept by God's power, so you can have real assurance, keep repenting when you fall, and not quit when doubts hit.

Key Bible passages (read these first)

- **John 10:27–30** - no one can snatch Jesus' sheep from His hand.
- **Romans 8:31–39** - nothing can separate believers from God's love in Christ.
- **Philippians 1:6** - God finishes what He starts.
- **1 John 2:19** - some leave because they were never truly of Christ.
- **Hebrews 3:12–14** - warnings that call us to keep trusting and obeying.

First, be clear about the question

The question is not, "Can a Christian drift for a season?"

A Christian can:

✝ stumble,

✝ fall into sin,

✝ feel dry,

✝ struggle with doubt,

✝ even go through a messy season.

The question is: **Can a true Christian finally and fully fall away from Christ forever?**

Many Christians answer: **No. God keeps His true people.** This is often called perseverance of the saints, or God's preserving grace.

Why many Christians believe God keeps His people

Here are three Bible-based reasons.

1) Jesus holds His sheep

In John 10, Jesus says His sheep hear His voice, He gives them eternal life, and they will never perish.

Then He says no one can snatch them from His hand.

That's strong.

If salvation depends on Jesus' grip, not your grip, that's good news.

2) Nothing can separate you from God's love

Romans 8 lists all kinds of threats—death, life, powers, present, future.

Then it says none of these can separate believers from God's love in Christ.

So your fear, your bad week, your stress, and even your enemies don't have the final say.

3) God finishes what He starts

Philippians 1:6 says God will bring His good work to completion.

That means salvation is not a half-done project God abandons.

So why does the Bible give warnings?

Hebrews gives real warnings.

These warnings are not fake.

They are one way God keeps His people.

A warning is like a guardrail on a mountain road.

The guardrail doesn't mean you're supposed to crash.

It helps keep you from crashing.

When a true Christian hears God's warnings, the Spirit uses them to wake them up and pull them back.

A helpful truth: there's a difference between stumbling and leaving

1 John 2:19 talks about people who left the faith and stayed gone.

It says they went out because they were not truly of us.

That doesn't mean we can always tell who is truly saved. God knows.

But it does show this: Some people are close to church life without being changed by Christ.

They like the group. They like the idea. They like the image.

Then they walk away when it gets hard.

Two big mistakes teens make here

Mistake 1: "I sinned, so I must not be saved"

A Christian can sin. Sadly, yes.

The question is not, "Do you ever sin?"

The question is:

- Do you repent, or do you make peace with sin?
- Do you return to Jesus, or do you run from Him?
- Do you want to obey, even while you struggle?

A tender conscience and a desire to come back to Christ can be a sign of real faith.

Mistake 2: "I prayed once, so I can live however I want"

That's dangerous.

If someone uses "eternal security" as an excuse to keep sin, they are not treating Jesus as Lord.

Real faith produces repentance and growth over time (not perfection, but direction).

How to handle doubt without spiraling

Doubt can come from different places:

- tiredness
- anxiety
- ongoing hidden sin
- being hurt by someone

✝ confusing teaching

✝ fear of not being "good enough"

Here are four steps that help.

Step 1: Look to Jesus, not your feelings

Feelings change fast.

Jesus doesn't.

Ask: "Am I trusting Jesus today?"

Even a small, honest trust is real.

Step 2: Confess known sin quickly

Hidden sin feeds doubt like fire feeds smoke.

If you're living a double life, assurance will feel far away.

Bring sin into the light:

✝ confess to God,

✝ talk with a trusted mature believer,

✝ take real steps to cut off temptation.

Step 3: Use God's means of growth

God often strengthens assurance through:

✝ Scripture,

✝ prayer,

✝ church,

✝ communion/Lord's Supper (in your church),

✝ fellowship.

Isolation makes doubt louder.

Step 4: Ask for help

Talk to a pastor, parent, or trusted leader.

You don't get extra points for struggling alone.

A simple "assurance check" (not a test to earn salvation)

Ask yourself:

1. Do I believe Jesus is the Savior and Lord?
2. Do I hate my sin, even when I fall into it?
3. Do I want to obey Jesus?
4. Do I return to God when I mess up?
5. Do I see any fruit over time (even small)?

If you can say yes in a real way, that can give comfort.

If you can't, don't fake it. Come to Jesus honestly. Repent and trust Him.

Real life: what to do this week if you're scared

Here's a calm plan:

- Read John 10:27–30 slowly.
- Pray: "Jesus, I want to be Your sheep. Help me hear Your voice."
- Confess any known sin.
- Tell a trusted adult what you're struggling with.
- Keep showing up to church and Scripture even when you don't feel it.

Faith is not mainly a feeling. It's a trust you choose.

Quick check (answer in your own words)

1. What does John 10 say Jesus gives His sheep?

2. Why does the Bible warn believers in places like Hebrews?

3. What is the difference between stumbling and walking away from Christ?

4. What is one next step you should take if you're doubting?

Memory verse

"I give them eternal life, and they shall never perish; no one will snatch them out of my hand." - John 10:28

Action step for the week

Do the "Hold On" plan for 6 days.

Each day:

1. Read one passage:
    o   Day 1: John 10:27–30
    o   Day 2: Romans 8:31–39
    o   Day 3: Philippians 1:3–11
    o   Day 4: 1 John 1:5–2:2
    o   Day 5: Hebrews 3:12–14
    o   Day 6: Psalm 23

2. Write two lines:
    o   **God promises:** (one promise from the text)

    ____

    ____

    o   **So I will:** (one response: repent, pray, talk to someone, obey)

    ____

    ____

Closing prayer

Father, I'm asking for steady faith. When I doubt, help me look to Jesus. Thank You that You are strong when I am weak. Show me my sin and help me repent. Give me assurance from Your Word and help me keep following Christ. Amen.

WEEK 35
Make Sense of Suffering
Where God Is When Life Hurts

Suffering can make you ask hard questions fast.

"Why is this happening?"

"Did God forget me?"

"Is God punishing me?"

"Why do bad people seem fine?"

"Why do I feel so alone?"

The Bible does not shame you for asking.

It also doesn't give you a fake answer.

It gives you something stronger: **God is present, God is wise, and God will finish His good plan.**

And it points you to Jesus, who suffered for you and walks with you.

The big idea

God is with you in suffering, uses it for wise purposes, and will make all things right, so you can trust Him and keep walking even when it hurts.

Key Bible passages (read these first)

- **Psalm 23** - God is with you in the valley.
- **Romans 8:18–39** - suffering now, glory later, and God's love holds you.
- **2 Corinthians 1:3–5** - God comforts us so we can comfort others.
- **James 1:2–4** - trials can produce endurance.
- **John 11:32–44** - Jesus weeps with the grieving, then acts.

First, name the truth: suffering is real

The Bible doesn't say, "Pain is an illusion."

It shows:

- † people crying,
- † people mourning,
- † people angry,
- † people confused,
- † people praying through tears.

So you don't have to pretend.

God can handle honest prayer.

Why suffering exists (without blaming God for evil)

The Bible gives a big reason:

Sin broke the world.

That's why:

- † bodies break,
- † relationships break,
- † injustice happens,
- † death happens.

Not all suffering is caused by your personal sin.

Sometimes you suffer because you live in a fallen world.

Sometimes you suffer because others sin.

Sometimes you suffer because you made a foolish choice.

But the Bible is clear: God is not evil, and He does not do wrong.

Where is God when life hurts?

Psalm 23 answers with a picture.

Even in the valley of the shadow of death, God is with you.

Notice it doesn't say you won't go through valleys.

It says you won't go through them alone.

God's presence is not always felt like a strong emotion.

Sometimes it's quiet strength:

- † you still get up,
- † you still pray,
- † you still keep going,
- † you still obey,
- † you still hope.

That's God holding you.

The strongest proof: Jesus suffered

If you ever think God can't relate, look at Jesus.

Jesus:

✝ was rejected,

✝ was betrayed,

✝ was mocked,

✝ was beaten,

✝ was crucified.

He knows pain from the inside.

And in John 11, Jesus weeps with people who are grieving.

That shows: God is not cold.

Then Jesus raises Lazarus.

That shows: God is not weak.

So in Jesus you see both:

✝ compassion,

✝ and power.

Is suffering always punishment?

Sometimes God disciplines His children, yes, because He loves them (Hebrews 12).

But not all suffering is punishment.

Jesus corrects this thinking in John 9 when people assume a man's suffering must be caused by his personal sin.

If you belong to Christ, your punishment for sin was taken by Jesus at the cross.

So when a Christian suffers, it's not God paying you back.

It may be:

✝ discipline,

✝ training,

✝ protection,

✝ shaping,

✝ or simply life in a broken world where God stays near.

What God can do through suffering

Romans 8 says God works all things for good for those who love Him.

That good is not always comfort.

Often God's good includes:

- deeper faith,
- stronger character,
- clearer priorities,
- greater compassion,
- less love for sin,
- more hope in the new creation.

James 1 says trials can produce endurance.

That doesn't make pain "nice."

It means pain can have purpose.

What to do when you don't understand

You don't need all the answers to take the next faithful step.

Here are five steady steps for suffering:

1) Tell God the truth

Pray honestly. Use the Psalms if you don't have words.

2) Ask for help

Ask God for comfort and strength. Ask people for support too.

3) Stay close to Scripture

When emotions are loud, Scripture is steady.

4) Don't isolate

Suffering can tempt you to disappear.

But God often comforts through His people.

5) Look ahead

Romans 8 says present suffering is not worth comparing to future glory.

That's not minimizing pain. It's giving hope a future.

Real life: teen situations where this matters

Suffering for teens can look like:

- parents fighting or divorcing
- anxiety or depression

- ✝ being bullied
- ✝ loneliness
- ✝ sickness in the family
- ✝ grief after a death
- ✝ betrayal by a friend
- ✝ pressure that feels too heavy

God sees all of it.

And He calls you to bring it to Him, not hide it.

Quick check (answer in your own words)

1. What does Psalm 23 teach you about God in suffering?

____

____

____

____

2. Why doesn't suffering always mean God is punishing you?

____

____

____

3. What is one way God can use suffering for good?

____

____

____

4. What is one next step you can take this week if you're hurting?

____

____

____

Memory verse

"Even though I walk through the darkest valley, I will fear no evil, for you are with me; your rod and your staff, they comfort me." - Psalm 23:4

Action step for the week

Do the "Valley Plan" for 6 days.

Each day:

1. Read **Psalm 23** slowly.

2. Write three short lines:
    o   **Today's valley is:** (name the pain or fear)

    ____

    ____

    o   **God is with me because:** (one phrase from Psalm 23)

    ____

    ____

    o   **So today I will:** (one step: pray, talk to someone, rest, obey, ask for help)

    ____

    ____

    ____

Then do one simple support step:

✝   tell a trusted adult what's going on,

✝   ask for prayer,

✝   or text a mature believer, "Can you pray for me today?"

Closing prayer

God, life hurts sometimes, and I don't always understand. Please stay near to me. Help me trust You in the valley. Give me comfort, wisdom, and strength. Thank You for Jesus who suffered for me and rose again. Help me keep walking with hope. Amen.

PART SEVEN
Belong to the Church

WEEK 36
Choose Community:
What the Church Is

When you hear "church," you might think of a building, a service, or a boring event your parents drag you to.

But in the Bible, the church is not mainly a place you go.

The church is a people God saves and gathers.

And if you follow Jesus, the church is not optional.

It's part of how God keeps you, grows you, and sends you.

The big idea

The church is God's people in Christ, so you should belong, grow with others, and live your faith as part of a family.

Key Bible passages (read these first)

- ✝ **Acts 2:42–47** - the early church's life together.
- ✝ **1 Corinthians 12:12–27** - the church is Christ's body.
- ✝ **Ephesians 2:19–22** - believers are God's household and His dwelling.
- ✝ **Hebrews 10:24–25** - don't neglect meeting together.

What the church is (simple definition)

The church is **all people who truly trust Jesus.**

That includes:

- ✝ the worldwide church (all believers everywhere), and
- ✝ local churches (a real group of believers you can know and join).

So the church is not:

- † a building,
- † a brand,
- † a concert,
- † a club for good people.

It is God's saved people, gathered around Jesus, living under His Word.

Why God created the church

God could save people and keep them alone.

But He doesn't.

He saves people into a family.

Here are four reasons the church exists.

1) Worship

Christians gather to worship God together.

Not because God needs applause, but because we need to remember who God is.

Worship resets your heart.

2) Teaching

Acts 2 says the early believers devoted themselves to the apostles' teaching.

The church is where you learn Scripture clearly and apply it to life.

3) Fellowship

Fellowship is not snacks after service.

It's sharing life: praying, helping, encouraging, correcting, caring.

4) Mission

The church isn't meant to be a holy bubble.

Jesus sends His people into the world with the gospel.

The church is a body, not a crowd

1 Corinthians 12 says believers are like parts of a body.

A body needs:

- † eyes,
- † hands,
- † feet,
- † ears.

Every part matters.

That means:

- you are needed,
- and you need others.

A body part cut off from the body doesn't become "more free."

It dies.

That's why "me and Jesus only" is not the Bible's plan.

"But church people hurt me"

This is real.

Churches are full of sinners being changed. That means you will see hypocrisy sometimes. You will see hurt sometimes.

But don't confuse Jesus with people who fail to act like Jesus.

Also remember: avoiding church doesn't heal the problem of sin.

It just removes you from one of God's main places of growth and care.

God often uses the church to:

- correct you,
- comfort you,
- protect you,
- and mature you.

If you've been wounded, it may take time to trust again. That's okay. But don't give up on Christ's church.

What you should expect from a healthy church

No church is perfect, but a healthy church will usually have:

- Bible teaching that matches Scripture
- worship that honors God, not fame
- love that shows up in actions
- leadership that serves, not controls
- discipline that protects, not shames
- a focus on the gospel, not just rules

If a church hides sin, protects abuse, or refuses correction, that's serious. In those cases, get help from trusted adults and wise leaders.

Real life: what church gives a teen

Here's what the church can give you that social media can't.

1) Real belonging

Not based on looks, status, or talent.

Belonging based on Christ.

2) Older Christians who can guide you

Teen life has big choices. You need wisdom beyond your own age group.

3) People who pray for you

When you're tired, others can carry you in prayer.

4) Chances to serve

You grow by giving, not only by receiving.

Quick check (answer in your own words)

1. What is the church, according to the Bible?

2. What's the difference between the worldwide church and a local church?

3. Why is "me and Jesus only" not God's plan?

4. What is one thing you need from the church right now: teaching, friendship, help, or accountability?

Memory verse

"And let us consider how we may spur one another on toward love and good deeds, not giving up meeting together, as some are in the habit of doing, but encouraging one another—and all the more as you see the Day approaching." - Hebrews 10:24–25

Action step for the week

Do one "choose community" step this week.

Pick one:

- Introduce yourself to one adult leader and learn their name.
- Join a youth group night or Bible study and stay after for five minutes.
- Ask one older Christian, "Can you pray for me this week?"
- Sit with someone who looks alone.
- Ask your parents or guardian: "How can I serve our church this month?"

Then write one sentence: **"This is how I showed up as part of Christ's body."**

Closing prayer

God, thank You for saving me into a family, not leaving me alone. Help me love the church the way You do. Give me courage to show up, to grow, and to serve. Protect our church and make us more like Jesus. Amen.

WEEK 37
Show Up as Family:
Why Membership Matters

Some teens think church membership is an "adult thing."

Or they hear the word "membership" and think of:

- ✝ a gym contract,
- ✝ signing papers,
- ✝ getting stuck.

But in the Bible, belonging to a local church is not about a label.

It's about **love with commitment.**

It's choosing to show up, be known, be cared for, and care for others, like family.

The big idea

Church membership is a committed way to belong to a local church, so you can be known, protected, discipled, and useful in Christ's body.

Key Bible passages (read these first)

- ✝ **Acts 2:41–47** - believers are added and live as a real community.
- ✝ **1 Corinthians 12:18–27** - you belong to a body with many parts.
- ✝ **Hebrews 13:17** - leaders watch over souls (that requires a known flock).
- ✝ **Galatians 6:1–2** - restore, carry burdens, and help each other grow.
- ✝ **Matthew 18:15–17** - the church helps with serious sin and restoration.

What "membership" means (in plain words)

Membership means you and a local church make a clear commitment:

You say: "These are my people. I will show up, follow Jesus with them, and use my life to build them up."

The church says: "We will care for you, teach you, guide you, correct you when needed, and treat you as family."

So membership is not about being on a list.

It's about being **known and committed.**

Why commitment matters (even for teens)

It's easy to float.

You can attend different places, never get close, never be challenged, and never be truly cared for.

That feels safe, but it can leave you weak.

Commitment matters because real growth needs:

- real relationships,
- real accountability,
- real care when life hurts.

Four reasons membership is a gift

1) Membership helps you be known

In a crowd, it's easy to hide.

Membership pushes you toward honest life:

- people know your name,
- your leaders know you exist,
- someone notices when you disappear.

That's not control. That's care.

2) Membership gives spiritual protection

Hebrews 13 says leaders watch over souls.

That only works if there's a clear "we":

- who the leaders are responsible for,
- and who is under their care.

A healthy church protects people from:

- false teaching,
- secret sin,
- spiritual isolation.

3) Membership helps you grow up in Christ

Galatians 6 says believers help restore one another and carry burdens.

That's family behavior.

When you're drifting, you need someone who will say, kindly: "Hey, I love you. What's going on?"

Membership creates a place where that kind of love is normal.

4) Membership helps you serve on purpose

A body works best when each part knows where it fits.

If you belong, you stop being a spectator.

You start asking: "Where can I help? What needs to be done? Who needs encouragement?"

"But I'm a teen, can I really be a member?"

That depends on your church's practice.

Some churches have youth membership with a process. Others wait until a certain age.

Either way, you can still live the heart of membership right now:

- ✝ be consistent,
- ✝ be known,
- ✝ be teachable,
- ✝ serve,
- ✝ stay accountable,
- ✝ treat the church like family.

So even if you can't officially join yet, you can belong in a real way.

What membership is NOT

Let's clear two worries.

Membership is not "I'm trapped"

A healthy church will never use membership to control you.

If a church uses fear or threats to keep people, that's a warning sign.

Membership is not "I'm perfect now"

Joining doesn't mean you have no struggles.

It means you're choosing to follow Jesus with help.

What to look for before committing

You don't need a perfect church, but you do need a church that is serious about Jesus.

Look for:

    ✝   Bible teaching that matches Scripture

    ✝   leaders with humble character

    ✝   a clear gospel message

    ✝   real care for people

    ✝   a willingness to correct sin and protect the vulnerable

If something feels unsafe, talk to trusted adults and wise leaders outside your peer group.

Real life: what "show up as family" looks like this week

Here are simple ways to practice membership heart-level, even as a teen.

    ✝   Sit with someone new.

    ✝   Learn one adult's name and ask how you can pray for them.

    ✝   Stay after church five minutes and talk to someone outside your usual group.

    ✝   Ask a leader, "What's one way I can serve?"

    ✝   If you miss church, don't ghost—message someone and stay connected.

Family doesn't disappear when it's inconvenient.

Quick check (answer in your own words)

1. In your own words, what is church membership?

2. Why does commitment help you grow?

3. What is one fear you have about being "known" at church?

    ____

    ____

    ____

4. What is one way you can show up like family this week?

    ____

    ____

    ____

Memory verse

"Carry each other's burdens, and in this way you will fulfill the law of Christ." - Galatians 6:2

Action step for the week

Do one "be known" step and one "serve" step.

Be known (pick one):

✝ Ask a leader: "Can I share something I'm struggling with?"

✝ Tell a trusted adult at church one way they can pray for you.

✝ Join a small group or stay for youth group discussion.

Serve (pick one):

✝ help set up or clean up,

✝ greet someone at the door,

✝ help with kids (with permission and safety rules),

✝ stack chairs,

✝ run slides,

✝ help someone carry something.

Then write one sentence:

"This week I treated the church like family by ________________

____

Closing prayer

Father, thank You for putting me in Your family through Jesus. Help me not live alone. Give me courage to be known and to show love with commitment. Help our church feel like a real family that tells the truth and cares well. Amen.

WEEK 38
Serve with Your Gifts:
How God Uses You

A lot of teens think church is something you attend.

Like a school assembly.

You sit, you listen, you leave.

But the Bible describes the church as a body where every part matters. That means God didn't save you only so you can "get fed."

He saved you so you can grow and also help others grow.

God has work for you to do.

Not to earn His love.

Because you already have His love in Christ.

The big idea

God gives every believer gifts and opportunities to serve, so you can build up the church, love people in real ways, and grow stronger faith.

Key Bible passages (read these first)

- ✝ **1 Corinthians 12:4-7, 12-27** — different gifts, one body, each part needed.

- ✝ **Romans 12:4-8** — gifts used with humble service.

- ✝ **1 Peter 4:10-11** — use your gift to serve others as a steward of God's grace.

- ✝ **Ephesians 2:10** — saved by grace for good works God prepared.

What spiritual gifts are (simple definition)

Spiritual gifts are **abilities God gives believers to serve the church and help others.**

They are not the same as talents, but they can overlap.

✝ A talent can be natural (music, sport, speaking).

✝ A spiritual gift is given by God for serving others in Christ.

The point is not, "Look how gifted I am."

The point is, "How can I help?"

Why God gives gifts

1 Corinthians 12 says gifts are given "for the common good."

That means gifts are not mainly for your own spotlight.

They're meant to build up the church.

So if God gave you something, it's for serving.

A few common gifts (with teen examples)

The Bible lists many gifts in different places. Here are a few, with simple examples of how teens can use them.

Serving / helps

You notice needs and jump in.

Examples:

✝ setting up chairs,

✝ helping with kids (with permission),

✝ cleaning,

✝ carrying equipment,

✝ running sound or slides.

Encouragement

You help people keep going.

Examples:

✝ texting someone Scripture when they're down,

✝ checking on a friend who's missing,

✝ thanking volunteers,

✝ encouraging younger kids.

Teaching

You can explain God's Word clearly.

Examples:

✝ helping in a younger class,

✝ leading a short discussion in youth group,

✝ helping a friend understand a passage.

Mercy

You care for hurting people with kindness.

Examples:

- sitting with the lonely kid,
- writing a card to someone sick,
- helping with food drives,
- showing patience with difficult people.

Giving / generosity

You share what you have to bless others.

Examples:

- giving a portion of allowance,
- helping someone who needs lunch money,
- donating clothes,
- sacrificing something you want to help someone else.

Leadership

You help a group move in a good direction.

Examples:

- organizing a service project,
- helping new teens feel included,
- setting a tone of respect and honesty.

Not everyone has the same gifts.

That's the point.

Two big lies that stop teens from serving

Lie 1: "I'm too young to matter"

Paul told Timothy not to let people despise him for his youth (1 Timothy 4:12).

God uses young believers.

You may not lead everything, but you can serve in real ways.

Lie 2: "If I serve, people will judge me"

Sometimes they might.

But serving is not about people clapping. It's about loving like Jesus.

Jesus washed feet.

Serving will humble you, and humility is good for your soul.

Serving helps you grow

Serving isn't only "helpful for the church."

It's also good for you.

Serving:

- fights selfishness,
- helps you notice others,
- builds courage,
- teaches responsibility,
- strengthens friendships,
- helps you find your place.

Many teens grow more in seasons of serving than seasons of only consuming.

How to find where you fit (no stress)

You don't need a perfect "calling moment."

Start simple.

Ask these four questions:

1. **What needs do I notice?**
2. **What service do I enjoy doing?**
3. **What do others say I'm good at?**
4. **What opportunities are available in my church right now?**

Then try something for a month.

If it's not a fit, try something else.

You're not locked in forever.

Serving the right way: two guardrails

Serving is good, but it can go wrong.

Guardrail 1: Serve with humility

Romans 12 warns against thinking too highly of yourself.

Gifts are gifts.

Stay humble.

Guardrail 2: Serve with healthy limits

You're still a teen.

School, family, and rest matter.

Serving should not replace sleep, obedience to parents, or mental health care.

Talk with your parents and leaders about a balanced schedule.

Real life: what serving can look like this week

Here are easy "first steps" for teens:

- Ask, "How can I help this Sunday?"
- Volunteer once a month in children's ministry (if allowed).
- Help with tech (sound, slides).
- Join a setup/cleanup team.
- Serve at a church outreach or food drive.
- Write encouragement notes for people who are sick or grieving.

Simple service is real service.

Quick check (answer in your own words)

1. What are spiritual gifts for?

____

____

____

____

2. What lie most stops you from serving?

____

____

____

3. What is one area in your church where you could help?

____

____

____

4. How can serving help your faith grow?

____

____

____

____

Memory verse

"Each of you should use whatever gift you have received to serve others, as faithful stewards of God's grace in its various forms." - 1 Peter 4:10

Action step for the week

Do the "One Month Serve" step.

1. Choose **one** way to serve for the next 4 weeks.
2. Tell a leader and your parent/guardian.
3. Show up and do it with a good attitude.

Then each week, write one sentence:

✝ **"This week I served by** _______________________________
   and learned_______________________________________

Keep it real. Keep it simple.

Closing prayer

God, thank You for saving me by grace and giving me a place in Your church. Show me how to serve. Give me humility, joy, and steady love for people. Use my life to build others up and honor Jesus. Amen.

WEEK 39
Follow Godly Leaders:
What Leadership Is For

Most teens have seen leadership go wrong.

A coach who yells and shames. A teacher who plays favorites. A politician who lies. Even a church leader who hurts people.

So it's normal to feel suspicious of leaders.

But the Bible doesn't say, "Forget leadership."

It says God gives leaders for the good of His people, when they lead like Jesus.

This week is about what church leadership is for, how to respond to it, and how to spot danger signs.

The big idea

God gives church leaders to serve, teach, and protect His people, so you can learn with humility, follow wisely, and speak up when something is wrong.

Key Bible passages (read these first)

- **Hebrews 13:17** - leaders watch over souls.
- **1 Peter 5:1-4** - leaders shepherd willingly, not for selfish gain.
- **1 Timothy 3:1-7** - character matters for leaders.
- **Acts 20:28-31** - leaders must guard the church from false teaching.
- **Mark 10:42-45** - Jesus defines leadership as serving, not controlling.

What church leadership is for

In Scripture, leaders are not celebrities.

They are shepherds.

A shepherd's job is not to look important. It's to care for the sheep.

Healthy church leadership usually includes these goals:

1) Teach God's Word

Leaders help the church understand Scripture and apply it.

They don't make up new messages. They explain God's message.

2) Protect the church

Acts 20 warns that false teachers will come.

Leaders guard the church by:

- correcting error,
- warning people,
- and keeping the gospel clear.

3) Care for people

Leaders pray, counsel, and help people grow.

They should notice needs and respond with love.

4) Set direction for mission

Leaders help the church stay focused on making disciples, not chasing trends.

The main test for leaders: character

1 Timothy 3 lists qualities for leaders. It focuses more on character than talent.

Godly leaders should be:

- self-controlled
- trustworthy
- gentle, not violent
- not greedy
- faithful at home
- respected for real reasons

This matters because a talented speaker can still be unsafe.

God cares who a leader is when no one is watching.

Jesus' definition of leadership

Mark 10 says leaders in the world often "lord it over" people.

Jesus says His followers must not lead that way.

In Jesus' kingdom, leadership is service.

Jesus proves it by giving His life.

So a godly leader will not use people.

They will serve people.

How you should respond to good leadership

Hebrews 13:17 says to obey and submit to leaders, because they watch over souls.

That can sound intense, so here's what it means in real life:

✝ You listen with humility.

✝ You take correction seriously.

✝ You don't treat leaders like enemies.

✝ You cooperate when they lead according to Scripture.

This does not mean leaders are always right.

It means you don't live in stubborn independence.

God often uses leaders to help you grow.

Your role matters too

Following well doesn't mean you stop thinking.

The Bible calls you to be wise.

Here are three healthy habits:

1) Be teachable

If you assume you already know everything, you won't grow.

Ask: "What can I learn here?"

2) Check teaching with Scripture

Acts 17:11 praises people who examined the Scriptures daily to see if teaching was true.

So it's okay to:

✝ take notes,

✝ read the passage,

✝ ask questions respectfully.

3) Pray for your leaders

Leading is heavy.

Pray for:

✝ courage,

✝ purity,

✝ wisdom,

✝ and protection from pride.

Warning signs of unhealthy leadership

This part is important. The Bible warns about leaders who harm people.

Be careful if you see patterns like:

✝ **Control:** "Don't question us. Just obey."

✝ **Secrecy:** no accountability, no transparency.

✝ **Fear tactics:** threats, shame, or pressure to stay quiet.

✝ **Money obsession:** constant pushing for cash, leaders living flashy.

✝ **Isolation:** discouraging you from getting outside help.

✝ **Cover-ups:** protecting abusers or ignoring sin to protect image.

If something feels unsafe, tell a trusted adult. If it involves abuse, report it to the proper authorities and get help right away.

Real life: what this looks like for teens

Here are normal ways to practice wise followership.

✝ Show respect, even when you disagree.

✝ Ask honest questions at the right time, with a calm tone.

✝ If you're corrected, don't rage or ghost. Think and pray.

✝ If you see a real problem, speak up to a safe adult and follow proper steps.

Following Jesus includes learning how to deal with authority in a wise, brave way.

Quick check (answer in your own words)

1. What is church leadership for, according to Scripture?

____

____

____

____

2. What matters more than talent in a leader?

____

____

____

3. What is one sign of healthy leadership?

____

____

____

____

4. What is one warning sign that should make you get help?

____

____

____

____

Memory verse

"Be shepherds of God's flock that is under your care, watching over them—not because you must, but because you are willing, as God wants you to be; not pursuing dishonest gain, but eager to serve; 3 not lording it over those entrusted to you, but being examples to the flock." -
1 Peter 5:2–3

Action step for the week

Do one "honor and help" step this week.

Pick one:

✝ Write a short note or text to a leader: "Thank you for serving our church."

✝ Ask a leader, "How can I pray for you this week?" Then actually pray.

✝ If you disagree with something, write your question down and ask respectfully in person (not as a public call-out).

Then write one sentence: **"This week I practiced wise followership by** ____

____

____

Closing prayer

God, thank You for giving leaders to Your church. Please give our leaders humble hearts and clean lives. Help me be teachable and wise. Protect me and my church from harmful leadership. Help us all follow Jesus, the true Shepherd. Amen.

WEEK 40
Handle Conflict Like Jesus
Forgive and Make Peace

Conflict is not rare.

It happens in families, friend groups, youth groups, sports teams, and group chats.

Sometimes you're the one who got hurt. Sometimes you're the one who did the hurting. Sometimes it's both.

The Bible doesn't say, "Avoid conflict at all costs."

It teaches you how to handle it like Jesus: with truth, humility, and forgiveness.

The big idea

Because Jesus forgave you, you can face conflict with truth and mercy, forgive from the heart, and pursue peace without pretending sin is fine.

Key Bible passages (read these first)

- ✝ **Matthew 18:15–17, 21–35** - how to deal with sin and why forgiveness matters.
- ✝ **Ephesians 4:31–32** - forgive as God forgave you in Christ.
- ✝ **Romans 12:17–21** - pursue peace; overcome evil with good.
- ✝ **Colossians 3:12–15** - put on compassion and let peace rule.
- ✝ **Proverbs 19:11** - wisdom can overlook some offenses.

First, be clear: conflict has different levels

Not every conflict is the same.

Some things are small. Some things are serious. Some things are unsafe.

So before you act, ask: "What kind of conflict is this?"

Here are three levels:

Level 1: Minor offenses (annoying, rude, thoughtless)

These are moments you can often overlook with wisdom (Proverbs 19:11).

Not every irritation needs a confrontation.

Level 2: Real sin that damages trust

This includes lying, gossip, disrespect, cruelty, and betrayal.

These are times when love may require a conversation.

Level 3: Unsafe situations

Abuse, threats, stalking, sexual harm, serious manipulation.

Forgiveness never means staying unsafe.

If you are in danger, get help right away from trusted adults and proper authorities.

Jesus' plan for conflict: Matthew 18

Jesus gives a simple path.

Step 1: Go privately first

"If your brother sins against you, go and tell him his fault, between you and him alone."

This protects people from public shame.

It also stops gossip.

So the first move is usually not:

- posting,
- blasting,
- telling ten friends.

It's a calm, private conversation.

Step 2: If they won't listen, bring one or two

This adds wisdom and fairness.

It also protects you if the other person twists the story.

Step 3: If it's still unresolved, involve the church

This is for serious and ongoing issues, not for petty drama.

It's about restoring, not crushing.

How to confront like Jesus (without being mean)

Use this simple sentence:

"When you did _______________________________, it hurt me
because ____ .
Can we talk about it?"

Keep it specific.

Don't bring a long list from three years ago.

Don't attack their character.

Talk about the action.

Then listen.

Sometimes the person didn't realize what they did.

Sometimes they did.

Either way, you're choosing truth over gossip.

What forgiveness is (and what it is not)

Forgiveness can feel confusing, so let's be clear.

Forgiveness is:

- releasing revenge to God,
- refusing to keep punishing the person in your heart,
- choosing to treat them with mercy, not hatred,
- praying for God to work.

Forgiveness is NOT:

- pretending it didn't happen,
- calling evil "fine,"
- trusting someone instantly,
- staying in unsafe situations,
- letting someone keep harming you.

Forgiveness is about your heart. Trust is about their actions over time.

You can forgive someone and still set strong boundaries.

Why forgiveness is possible

Ephesians 4:32 says forgive one another as God forgave you in Christ.

That means your forgiveness is rooted in the gospel.

You forgive not because the other person earned it.

You forgive because Jesus forgave you.

This protects you from bitterness.

Bitterness feels powerful, but it slowly poisons you.

Forgiveness is a way out.

What if the person won't apologize?

You can still forgive.

Forgiveness is not the same as reconciliation.

Reconciliation requires:

- repentance,
- truth,
- and rebuilding trust.

If the person refuses to own their sin, you can:

- release revenge,
- set boundaries,
- and keep your heart free from hate.

Romans 12 says, as far as it depends on you, live at peace with all.

Sometimes peace means: "I will not keep fighting, but I won't pretend everything is okay."

A teen-level problem: group chat conflict

Group chats can turn small issues into big fires fast.

If you want to follow Jesus in conflict, avoid these traps:

- screenshot wars
- public roasting
- vague-posting
- spreading "your side" first

Instead:

- pause before you respond,
- talk privately,
- ask a leader or parent for help if it's messy.

Real life: a "Peace Plan" you can use

Here is a simple plan for most conflicts (not unsafe ones).

1) Pray first (one sentence)

"God, help me tell the truth with love."

2) Check your own heart

Ask:

- ☐ "Am I angry because my pride was hit?"
- ☐ "Did I sin too?"

If yes, own your part.

3) Choose the right level

Overlook, talk privately, or get help.

4) Speak calmly and clearly

No exaggeration. No insults.

5) Forgive from the heart

Release revenge to God.

6) Set wise boundaries

Forgive does not mean "act like nothing happened."

Quick check (answer in your own words)

1. What are the three levels of conflict?

2. What is Jesus' first step in Matthew 18?

3. What is forgiveness, and what is it not?

4. What is one conflict you need to handle more like Jesus?

Memory verse

"Be kind and compassionate to one another, forgiving each other, just as in Christ God forgave you." -
Ephesians 4:32

Action step for the week

Do one "peace step" in the next 7 days.

Pick one:

- ✝ Apologize for a wrong you did (no excuses).
- ✝ Forgive someone in prayer and stop replaying the offense.
- ✝ Have a private talk using the sentence:

  When you did ____

  it hurt because _____________________________________

- ✝ Leave a gossip conversation and refuse to spread drama.
- ✝ If the conflict is unsafe, tell a trusted adult and ask for help immediately.

Then write one sentence:

"This week I pursued peace by　　　."

Closing prayer

Jesus, thank You for forgiving me. Help me handle conflict with truth and kindness. Guard my heart from bitterness and revenge. Give me courage to apologize when I am wrong and wisdom to set boundaries when needed. Make me a peacemaker. Amen.

PART EIGHT
Practice the Faith

WEEK 41
Pray with Boldness:
Talk to God Like It's Real

A lot of teens feel weird about prayer.

Some feel like they don't know the right words. Some feel like God is far away. Some feel guilty, so they avoid God. Some only pray when they're scared.

But prayer is not a performance.

Prayer is talking to the real God who hears you because of Jesus.

You don't pray boldly because you're brave.

You pray boldly because God is good, and Jesus opened the way.

The big idea

Because Jesus brings you to God, you can pray honestly and boldly, trusting that God hears you and helps you.

Key Bible passages (read these first)

- **Matthew 6:9–13** - Jesus teaches the Lord's Prayer.
- **Hebrews 4:14–16** - come to God's throne with confidence.
- **Philippians 4:6–7** - pray instead of panic; God gives peace.
- **Romans 8:26–27** - the Spirit helps you when you don't know what to say.
- **Psalm 62:8** - pour out your heart to God.

What "bold" prayer means

Bold prayer does not mean loud prayer.

It means confident prayer.

Hebrews 4 says you can come with confidence because Jesus is your High Priest.

So bold prayer means:

✝ you don't have to clean yourself up first,

✝ you don't have to impress God,

✝ you don't have to hide your real feelings.

You can come honestly.

The biggest barrier to prayer: thinking God is annoyed

Many teens picture God like an irritated adult: "Here we go again."

But Jesus teaches you to pray "Our Father."

That means God is not only Judge.

In Christ, He is your Father.

A good father listens.

A good father cares.

A good father corrects, yes, but he doesn't ignore his child's cry.

The Lord's Prayer: a simple prayer map

Jesus gives a model prayer, not a magic script.

Here's what it teaches you to pray about:

1) God's name

"Father, help me honor You."

Prayer starts with worship, not selfishness.

2) God's kingdom

"Your kingdom come."

This means: "God, rule my life. Fix what's broken. Save people."

3) Daily needs

"Give us this day our daily bread."

God cares about real needs:

✝ school stress,

✝ friendships,

✝ food,

✝ health,

✝ family problems,

✝ anxiety.

You're not bothering Him.

4) Forgiveness

"Forgive us... as we forgive."

Prayer includes confession and a forgiving heart.

5) Help in temptation

"Lead us not into temptation."

Prayer is part of fighting sin.

It's asking God for help before you fall.

When you don't know what to say

Romans 8 says the Spirit helps you in weakness.

That means:

- you can pray short prayers,
- you can pray messy prayers,
- you can pray with tears,
- you can pray with one sentence.

God is not grading grammar.

He is hearing His child.

Simple prayers are real prayers:

- "God, help me."
- "God, forgive me."
- "God, give me wisdom."
- "God, give me courage."
- "God, hold me."

What prayer does (and doesn't do)

Prayer is not a button that forces God.

Prayer is trust.

God answers prayer in wise ways:

- sometimes yes,
- sometimes no,
- sometimes wait,
- sometimes different than you expected.

But prayer is never wasted, because prayer connects you to God.

Even when the situation doesn't change fast, you change:

✝ your fear softens,

✝ your mind clears,

✝ your heart steadies,

✝ your faith grows.

Philippians 4 says prayer leads to God's peace guarding your heart and mind.

Real life: how to make prayer part of your day

If you only pray when you feel "spiritual," you won't pray much.

Try tying prayer to a habit you already do.

✝ when you wake up: "God, lead me today."

✝ before school: "God, help me obey You today."

✝ before meals: quick thanks

✝ when tempted: "Holy Spirit, help me say no."

✝ before sleep: confession and gratitude

Short prayers throughout the day build a real prayer life.

A healthy warning: don't turn prayer into show

Jesus warns against praying to be seen.

Prayer is not for points.

If you pray in public, keep it simple and sincere.

God cares about the heart.

Quick check (answer in your own words)

1. Why can you pray with confidence, according to Hebrews 4?

____

____

____

____

2. What are the five parts of the Lord's Prayer model?

____

____

____

____

3. What do you do when you don't know what to say?

____

____

____

____

4. What is one habit you can connect prayer to this week?

____

____

____

____

Memory verse

"Let us then approach God's throne of grace with confidence, so that we may receive mercy and find grace to help us in our time of need." - Hebrews 4:16

Action step for the week

Use the "5-Part Prayer" for 6 days.

Each day, pray one short line for each part:

1. **Praise:** "God, You are _________________________."
2. **Kingdom:** "Rule my _________________________ today."
3. **Needs:** "Please help with _________________________."
4. **Forgive:** "Forgive me for _________________________."
5. **Help:** "Help me resist _________________________."

Keep it under two minutes if you want. The goal is consistency, not length.

Closing prayer

Father, thank You that I can come to You because of Jesus. Teach me to pray honestly. Help me trust that You hear me. Give me peace when I'm anxious and strength when I'm tempted. Make prayer real in my daily life. Amen.

WEEK 42
Think Before You Act:
Wisdom for Choices and Temptation

A lot of regret starts with one sentence:

"I wasn't thinking."

You were tired. You were mad. You were bored. You wanted to fit in. You wanted relief. You wanted attention. You wanted control.

So you clicked. You texted. You snapped. You lied. You went along.

Wisdom is learning to slow down and choose the right path on purpose.

Wisdom is not being the smartest person in the room.

Wisdom is fearing God and living like His Word is true.

The big idea

Wisdom means choosing God's way before emotions and pressure choose for you, so you can avoid regret and walk in peace.

Key Bible passages (read these first)

- **Proverbs 1:7** - wisdom begins with fearing the Lord.
- **Proverbs 4:23–27** - guard your heart and keep your path straight.
- **James 1:5** - ask God for wisdom and He gives it.
- **James 1:14–15** - temptation grows from desire to sin to death.
- **Psalm 119:9–11** - God's Word helps you fight sin.

What wisdom is (simple)

Wisdom is **skill for living God's way.**

It means you don't only ask, "Can I do this?"

You ask better questions:

- ✝ "Should I do this?"
- ✝ "Will this help my faith?"
- ✝ "Will this pull me toward sin?"
- ✝ "Will this honor Jesus?"

Proverbs says wisdom starts with fearing the Lord.

That means God's opinion matters most.

Why temptation feels strong

Temptation is not always loud.

Often it sounds reasonable.

James 1 says temptation works like a hook:

- ✝ desire pulls you,
- ✝ then sin is born,
- ✝ then it grows,
- ✝ then it brings death.

So temptation usually starts earlier than the moment you "mess up."

It starts with what you desire and what you keep feeding.

The "pause" that changes everything

Wisdom builds a pause between feeling and acting.

Temptation wants speed.

Wisdom slows down.

You can learn to say: "Wait. What is happening in me right now?"

That pause can save you from a lot of pain.

A simple tool: the WISE check

Before a big choice, or a tempting moment, run this quick check.

- ✝ **W - What do I want right now?**

  Name it: approval, comfort, control, revenge, pleasure.

- ✝ **I - Is this wise according to Scripture?**

  Not "Do my friends approve?" but "Does God approve?"

- ✝ **S - Who should I speak to?**

  A parent, pastor, leader, or mature Christian.

- ✝ **E - What is the end of this path?**

  If I keep doing this, where will I be in 3 months?

This takes 20 seconds. It can save you years of regret.

Wisdom for daily decisions (not just "big sins")

Proverbs 4 says guard your heart and watch your path.

That includes small choices that shape you:

- what you watch "for fun"
- what you laugh at
- who you follow online
- what you do when you're bored
- what friends you let shape you
- what you do when no one is watching

Small choices build the kind of person you become.

Five practical wisdom habits for teens

1) Ask God for wisdom early

James 1:5 says God gives wisdom generously.

Don't wait until you're already in trouble.

Pray at the start of the day: "God, make me wise today."

2) Don't make big choices in a hot emotion

Angry choices usually hurt people. Lonely choices often lead to attention-seeking sin. Tired choices often lead to giving in.

If you're emotional, do a "cool-down" first:

- drink water,
- step outside,
- take 10 minutes,
- pray one sentence,
- then decide.

3) Guard your inputs

Psalm 119 says God's Word helps keep you clean.

What you feed your mind will feed your desires.

If your inputs are filled with lust, pride, and cruelty, your heart will lean that way.

If your inputs are filled with Scripture, truth, and wise voices, you'll be stronger.

4) Set "no" choices ahead of time

Don't decide in the moment.

Decide early:

- ✝ "I won't be alone with my phone late at night."
- ✝ "I won't flirt with someone else's boyfriend or girlfriend."
- ✝ "I won't join in gossip."
- ✝ "I won't cheat, even if I'm stressed."

Early decisions make later temptations weaker.

5) Choose friends who make obedience easier

Friends don't control you, but they shape you.

If your closest circle laughs at sin, it will be harder to be wise.

If your closest circle wants to follow Jesus, wisdom becomes more normal.

When you mess up: wisdom after failure

Wisdom doesn't mean "I never fall."

Wisdom means you respond the right way when you fall.

1. Confess quickly to God.
2. Own your choice (no blame).
3. Make it right if you harmed someone.
4. Cut off what fed the fall.
5. Ask for help so it doesn't stay secret.

Quick repentance is wisdom.

Quick check (answer in your own words)

1. What is wisdom, according to Proverbs 1:7?

   ____

   ____

   ____

   ____

2. What does James 1 say temptation grows from?

   ____

   ____

   ____

   ____

3. What is one situation where you need a "pause" before you act?

____

____

____

____

4. Which part of the WISE check will help you most this week?

____

____

____

____

Memory verse

"The fear of the Lord is the beginning of knowledge, but fools despise wisdom and instruction." - Proverbs 1:7

Action step for the week

Use the WISE check once per day for 6 days.

Each day, pick one real decision (small or big) and write four short lines:

- ✝ **W:** What I wanted was ______________________________ .
- ✝ **I:** Scripture says/teaches ______________________________ .
- ✝ **S:** I talked to / should talk to ______________________________ .
- ✝ **E:** If I keep going this way, it leads to ______________________ .

Then choose one wise action right away.

Closing prayer

God, give me wisdom. Help me fear You more than people. Help me slow down before I act. Show me the end of wrong paths. Strengthen me to choose what is right, even when temptation feels strong. Amen.

WEEK 43
Use Your Body God's Way: Purity, Dating, and Self-Control

Your body is not a joke.

It's not just a tool for pleasure. It's not a product to show off. It's not something you can treat like it has no meaning.

God made your body on purpose.

And if you belong to Jesus, your body belongs to Him too.

That sounds strict until you see God's heart: He wants to protect you, grow you, and help you love people the right way.

The big idea

Because your body belongs to God, you can honor Him with purity, date with wisdom, and practice self-control by the Holy Spirit's help.

Key Bible passages (read these first)

- ✝ **1 Corinthians 6:18–20** - your body is a temple of the Holy Spirit; glorify God in your body.
- ✝ **1 Thessalonians 4:3–8** - God's will is your sanctification; control your body in holiness.
- ✝ **Matthew 5:27–30** - Jesus calls for serious action against lust.
- ✝ **2 Timothy 2:22** - flee youthful passions and pursue righteousness.
- ✝ **Song of Solomon 8:4** - don't stir up love before the right time.

Start here: purity is bigger than "don't do stuff"

Purity is not only about avoiding one big sin.

Purity is about having a clean heart that honors God and respects people.

Purity means:
- you don't use people,
- you don't treat bodies like toys,
- you don't feed lust,
- you don't play games with someone's emotions,
- you don't flirt with sin and call it harmless.

Purity is love with self-control.

Why God cares about sexual sin

1 Corinthians 6 says sexual sin is serious and personal.

Why?

Because sex is not just physical.

It connects people. It shapes hearts. It creates deep memories. It can bring deep wounds when it's treated lightly.

God's commands are not meant to steal joy.

They are meant to protect real love.

Your body belongs to God

1 Corinthians 6 says you are not your own, for you were bought with a price.

That price is Jesus' blood.

So your body matters.

That means:
- what you watch matters,
- what you do in secret matters,
- how you touch others matters,
- how you talk about others matters.

This isn't about fear. It's about worship.

Purity in your mind: the first battlefield

Jesus said lust is not only a physical act. It starts in the heart.

That means purity includes your thought life.

You can't always control what pops into your mind.

But you can control what you feed and what you keep replaying.

A simple rule: **You can't stop every bird from flying over your head, but you can stop it from building a nest.**

So when a lustful thought shows up:

- name it as temptation,
- turn your mind toward what is true,
- move your body (stand up, leave, change the setting),
- ask God for help.

Porn is not "private"

Many teens think porn is a secret struggle that only affects them.

It doesn't.

Porn trains your brain to:

- treat people as objects,
- want more extreme content over time,
- compare real people to fake images,
- chase selfish pleasure instead of real love.

It also feeds shame, lying, and isolation.

If porn is part of your life, hear this clearly: You are not beyond grace. But you do need help, not just guilt.

What to do if you're stuck in porn or sexual sin

Here is a wise, clear plan. It's not magic, but it works over time.

1. **Confess to God** (no excuses).
2. **Tell a trusted adult** (parent, pastor, youth leader).
3. **Cut off easy access**
   - filters/accountability software if possible
   - no phone in bedroom at night
   - remove apps that feed temptation
4. **Replace the habit**
   - Scripture, prayer, exercise, serving, sleep
5. **Expect a fight**
   - temptation may spike at first
   - keep going anyway

Sin grows in darkness. Healing grows in light.

Dating with wisdom (not with games)

Dating can be good, but it's not a toy.

It's two image-bearers learning how to treat each other with honor.

If you're dating (or thinking about it), ask these questions:

1. Do we help each other follow Jesus or pull each other away?

____

____

2. Do we respect boundaries, or do we keep pushing?

____

____

3. Are we honest, or are we acting for attention?

____

____

4. Are we hiding this relationship, or is it open and wise?

____

____

5. Are we moving too fast emotionally or physically?

____

____

If a relationship pulls you into sin, it's not worth it.

Boundaries are not lack of love

Boundaries are love with wisdom.

Good boundaries protect both people.

Examples of wise boundaries:

- don't be alone in private places
- set a curfew
- avoid late-night texting that turns emotional fast
- don't lie to parents or leaders
- decide ahead of time what physical affection is off-limits

A boundary is a decision you make while you're calm, so you don't get trapped when you're tempted.

Self-control: the Spirit helps you

Self-control is part of the fruit of the Spirit (Galatians 5:23).

That means self-control is not you becoming a robot.

It's you becoming free.

Free from being pushed around by:

- cravings,
- pressure,
- emotions,
- "in the moment" choices.

Self-control grows by practice, like a muscle.

Every time you say no to temptation, you get stronger.

Even if you fail sometimes, don't quit. Repent and keep training.

Important safety note

If anyone pressures you, threatens you, touches you without consent, or makes you feel unsafe, that is serious.

That is not love.

Tell a trusted adult right away. Get help.

God cares about your safety and your dignity.

Quick check (answer in your own words)

1. What does 1 Corinthians 6 say about your body?

____

____

____

____

2. Why is purity bigger than "don't do certain acts"?

____

____

____

3. What is one situation where you need stronger boundaries?

____

____

____

4. What is one step you can take this week toward self-control?

____

____

____

____

Memory verse

*"Do you not know that your bodies are temples of the
Holy Spirit, who is in you, whom you have received from
God? You are not your own; you were bought at a price.
Therefore honor God with your bodies." -
1 Corinthians 6:19–20*

Action step for the week

Do the "Purity Plan" for 7 days.

Each day, write four short lines:

1. **My biggest temptation is:** _______________________________
2. **My top trigger is:** ___________________________________
   (bored, lonely, late night, stress, certain apps)
3. **My escape step is:** ___________________________________
   (leave room, block, put phone away, text a mentor)
4. **My replacement step is:** ______________________________
   (prayer, Scripture, walk, sleep, serving)

Then do one real boundary change this week:

✝ move your phone charging spot,

✝ remove an app,

✝ set a time limit,

✝ talk to a trusted adult,

✝ stop being alone with temptation.

Closing prayer

God, thank You for making my body and calling it good. Forgive me
for the ways I've misused my body or my mind. Please help me live with
purity and self-control. Give me courage to set boundaries and ask for
help. Make me someone who honors You and respects others. Amen.

WEEK 44
Tell the Truth:
Why Honesty Builds Trust

Lies feel useful in the moment.

They can protect your image. They can avoid trouble. They can make you look better. They can keep peace for a minute.

But lies always cost more than they promise.

They break trust.

And once trust breaks, it takes time to rebuild.

God calls His people to be truth-tellers because God is a God of truth.

The big idea

God calls you to tell the truth because He is true, so you can build trust, keep a clean conscience, and live with integrity.

Key Bible passages (read these first)

- **Ephesians 4:25** - put away falsehood; speak truth because we belong to one another.
- **Proverbs 12:22** - lying lips are an abomination; the faithful delight God.
- **Colossians 3:9–10** - don't lie; you've put on the new self.
- **John 14:6** - Jesus is the truth.
- **Matthew 5:37** - let your "yes" be yes and your "no" be no.

Why honesty matters to God

Honesty isn't just "good manners."

It's about who God is.

God does not lie.

God keeps His word.

God's promises are solid.

So when Christians lie, they act like their Father is not true.

Truth-telling is part of living like you belong to Jesus.

Lies are more than words

Lying is not only speaking something false.

Lying also includes:

- leaving out key truth to trick someone,
- twisting a story to look innocent,
- using half-truths to hide sin,
- pretending online,
- acting holy in public while living another life in private.

Any time you make someone believe something untrue on purpose, that's deceit.

Why teens lie (real reasons)

Most teens don't lie because they love evil.

They lie because they're trying to survive.

Common reasons:

- fear of punishment
- fear of disappointing parents
- fear of losing friends
- fear of embarrassment
- wanting attention
- wanting control

God understands your fear.

But God still calls you to truth.

Because truth is the path to freedom.

What lies do to you

Lies don't only hurt relationships.

They hurt you too.

1) Lies train your heart to hide

You start living in "image mode."

Always managing what people think.

That's exhausting.

2) Lies grow

One lie usually needs another lie to cover it.

Then another.

Then another.

3) Lies kill peace

Even if no one finds out, you know.

A guilty conscience steals rest.

What truth does

Truth does the opposite.

1) Truth builds trust

Trust grows when your words match reality.

Parents trust you more. Friends trust you more. Leaders trust you more.

2) Truth strengthens your conscience

You can sleep.

You don't have to keep a story straight.

3) Truth honors Jesus

Jesus is the truth.

When you speak truth, you reflect Him.

"But what if telling the truth gets me in trouble?"

Sometimes it will.

That's the hard part.

But trouble with truth is better than peace with lies.

Also, telling the truth early usually brings smaller consequences than lying and getting caught later.

And when you belong to Jesus, your goal is not "never get in trouble."

Your goal is to please God and live clean.

How to tell the truth when it's hard (a simple plan)

Use this five-step plan when you need to come clean.

Step 1: Pray one sentence

"God, help me tell the truth."

Step 2: Say it clearly

Don't soften it with tricks.

Say what happened.

Step 3: Own it

No blame shifting.

No "but they made me."

Step 4: Ask forgiveness

If you lied or hurt someone, say:

 "Will you forgive me?"

Step 5: Accept consequences

Honesty includes facing what comes next.

This is how trust gets rebuilt.

What about "kindness" and "truth" together?

Some teens use "honesty" as an excuse to be cruel.

That's not biblical.

Truth without love becomes harsh.

Love without truth becomes fake.

God calls you to both: speak truth **with** love (Ephesians 4:15).

So before you speak, ask:

- ✠ "Is this true?"
- ✠ "Is this needed?"
- ✠ "Is my goal to help or to hurt?"

Real life: honesty in a digital world

Online life can train you to fake things.

- ✠ filters that create a false image
- ✠ stories that hide your real life
- ✠ exaggerations for laughs
- ✠ fake confidence
- ✠ lying by omission in DMs

A simple teen rule: **Don't let your online self become a lie.**

You don't have to share everything.

But don't build a fake life.

Quick check (answer in your own words)

1. Why does God care about honesty?

   ____

   ____

   ____

   ____

2. What are two ways people lie without using obvious false words?

   ____

   ____

   ____

   ____

3. What does lying do to trust?

   ____

   ____

   ____

   ____

4. What is one truth you need to tell this week?

   ____

   ____

   ____

Memory verse

> *"Therefore each of you must put off falsehood and speak truthfully to your neighbor, for we are all members of one body." - Ephesians 4:25*

Action step for the week

Do the "Truth Practice" for 6 days.

Each day, choose one small honesty step:

- ✝ admit a mistake instead of making excuses
- ✝ correct a small exaggeration
- ✝ confess a lie quickly (within 24 hours)
- ✝ speak a hard truth kindly
- ✝ refuse to join gossip
- ✝ keep a promise you made

At the end of each day, write one sentence:

"Today I told the truth by____________________________ **."**

If you need to confess a bigger lie, don't wait.

Truth gets harder the longer you hold it.

Closing prayer

God of truth, forgive me for lying and hiding. Help me love truth more than my image. Give me courage to tell the truth even when it costs me something. Help me speak truth with love and build trust with my life. Amen.

WEEK 45
Work Hard with Joy:
School, Jobs, and Faithfulness

A lot of teens think faith is mostly about church stuff.

But God cares about your Monday.

He cares about your homework, your chores, your part-time job, your practice, and your attitude when no one is clapping.

Work is not a punishment.

Work is one way you honor God and love people.

The big idea

Because you belong to Jesus, you can work hard with joy and honesty, even when work feels boring or unfair.

Key Bible passages (read these first)

- **Colossians 3:23-24** - work heartily for the Lord, not for people.
- **Proverbs 6:6-11** - learn from the ant; don't be lazy.
- **Ephesians 6:5-8** - serve sincerely, as you would serve Christ.
- **2 Thessalonians 3:10-12** - don't live in idleness; do honest work.
- **Proverbs 11:1** - God cares about honesty in business.

Work matters to God

From the start, God gave humans work to do (Genesis 1-2).

Sin made work harder (Genesis 3), but work itself is still good.

Work is one way you:

- use what God gave you,
- help people,
- and learn faithfulness.

So school is not just "a thing you survive."

It is part of your life with God.

The difference between working hard and working for approval

Some teens work hard because they want to honor God.

Others work hard because they need to feel worthy.

Those are not the same.

Working for approval says: "If I do well, I matter."

Working for the Lord says: "I matter because I belong to Jesus, so I will be faithful."

Colossians 3 helps you shift your reason.

Three lies teens believe about work

Lie 1: "Work doesn't matter if it's not my dream"

Wrong.

Faithfulness matters in small tasks.

God often trains you in boring work before bigger work.

Lie 2: "If no one sees it, it doesn't count"

Wrong.

God sees.

Hidden faithfulness is still faithfulness.

Lie 3: "Cheating is fine if I need to keep up"

Wrong.

Cheating trades long-term character for short-term results.

God cares about honesty more than grades.

What "work heartily" looks like as a teen

1) In school

Working hard can look like:

- starting earlier instead of cramming at midnight,
- asking for help before you're failing,
- doing your own work,
- turning things in on time,
- paying attention even when class is dull.

This is not about being perfect.

It's about being faithful.

2) At home

Chores are training.

When you do chores without complaining (or with less complaining), you practice:

- ✦ humility,
- ✦ service,
- ✦ and self-control.

That is real spiritual growth.

3) At a job

If you have a job, your work is part of your witness.

Show up on time. Do what you said you would do. Don't steal time by scrolling. Don't trash your boss behind their back.

Your integrity preaches even when you don't say a word.

How to work with joy when you don't feel it

Joy is not the same as hype.

Joy is a steady gladness rooted in God.

Here are four ways to work with joy:

1) Remember who you serve

Colossians 3 says you serve the Lord Christ.

Even if your teacher is unfair, even if your coach is tough, even if your manager is annoying, God is still your true Master.

2) Do the next right thing

Don't wait to "feel motivated."

Do the next small step:

- ✦ open the book,
- ✦ write the first sentence,
- ✦ wash the first dish,
- ✦ clock in and start.

Small steps break lazy spirals.

3) Ask for help

Wisdom includes asking.

Talk to:

- a teacher,
- a tutor,
- a parent,
- a leader.

Pride says, "I have to handle it alone."

Faith says, "I'll get help and keep going."

4) Keep your life clean

Hidden sin drains energy.

A double life makes everything heavier.

Confess sin. Walk in the light. It helps more than you think.

When hard work turns into an idol

Work becomes an idol when:

- grades control your mood,
- success becomes your identity,
- you can't rest,
- you look down on others,
- you feel worthless when you fail.

God wants you to work hard, but also to trust Him more than results.

Your worth is not your report card.

Quick check (answer in your own words)

1. What does Colossians 3 say about who you work for?

   ____

   ____

   ____

   ____

2. What is one lie you believe about work?

   ____

   ____

   ____

   ____

3. Where do you struggle most: laziness, fear, or people-pleasing?

____

____

____

____

4. What is one faithful step you can take this week in school, home, or work?

____

____

____

____

Memory verse

"Whatever you do, work at it with all your heart, as working for the Lord, not for human masters," -
Colossians 3:23

Action step for the week

Do the "Faithful Work Plan" for 6 days.

Each day, write three short lines:

1. **Today's main task is:** _________________________________

2. **The temptation is:** _________________________________
    (procrastinate, cheat, complain, quit)

3. **For Jesus, I will:** ______________________ (one clear action)

Examples:

✝ "For Jesus, I will start my assignment before 7 p.m."

✝ "For Jesus, I will study 25 minutes without my phone."

✝ "For Jesus, I will do my chore without arguing."

Then do it the same day.

Closing prayer

God, thank You for the work You give me. Forgive me for laziness and complaining. Help me work hard with honesty and joy. Help me remember I serve Jesus in school, at home, and at work. Make me faithful in small things. Amen.

WEEK 46
Use Money and Stuff Wisely: Contentment and Generosity

Money is not just an "adult topic."

Teens deal with money and stuff all the time:

✝ clothes

✝ phones

✝ food

✝ brands

✝ online shopping

✝ allowance

✝ part-time jobs

✝ birthday money

And there's pressure everywhere to want more.

God doesn't hate money.

But God does warn you: money is a powerful tool, and it makes a terrible god.

The big idea

God calls you to be content and generous, so money and stuff don't control you, and you can honor Jesus with what you have.

Key Bible passages (read these first)

✝ **1 Timothy 6:6–10, 17–19** - be content; don't set hope on riches; be generous.

✝ **Matthew 6:19–24** - treasure in heaven; you can't serve two masters.

✝ **Hebrews 13:5** - be content; God will not leave you.

- ✝ **Proverbs 11:24-25** - generosity leads to blessing; the generous are refreshed.
- ✝ **2 Corinthians 9:6-8** - God loves a cheerful giver.

What contentment is

Contentment is not "I don't care about anything."

Contentment is a calm heart that says: "God has given me what I need today. I can thank Him and obey Him."

Contentment doesn't mean you never want to improve your life.

It means you don't need stuff to feel okay.

Why contentment is hard for teens

Because comparison is loud.

You see what others have:

- ✝ better shoes
- ✝ nicer phone
- ✝ cooler room
- ✝ more money
- ✝ more trips
- ✝ more "options"

Then your heart starts saying:

"If I had that, I'd be happy."

But happiness built on stuff never stays.

There's always a new thing to want.

The danger: money can become a master

Jesus says you can't serve two masters.

That means money isn't neutral.

Money will either be:

- ✝ a tool you use for God's purposes, or
- ✝ a master that uses you.

Here are signs money is becoming your master:

- ✝ you feel jealous a lot
- ✝ you obsess over brands
- ✝ you lie to get what you want
- ✝ you waste money to impress people

✝ you can't be happy for others

✝ you panic when you don't have enough

"The love of money" is the issue

1 Timothy 6 does not say money is evil.

It says **the love of money** is dangerous.

Love of money means:

✝ "Money will save me."

✝ "Money will make me safe."

✝ "Money will make me matter."

That's a lie.

Only God can give you real security.

How generosity breaks greed

Generosity is one of God's best tools to free your heart.

When you give, you're saying: "Money doesn't own me."

You're also copying God, who gives.

God gave His Son.

So Christians give because we've been given so much.

What generosity can look like for teens

Generosity is not only big donations.

It can be simple and real:

✝ buying a friend lunch who forgot money

✝ giving part of your allowance to missions or church

✝ saving up to bless someone in need

✝ sharing your stuff without being forced

✝ giving your time (time is valuable too)

✝ helping your family without charging for every little thing

Generosity is a habit, not a one-time moment.

Money wisdom for everyday teen life

Here are five wise rules you can start using now.

1) Give first

If you get money (allowance, job, gifts), choose a set amount to give first.

Even a small percent is a real start.

2) Save something

Saving is not selfish. It's wise.

Saving helps you avoid panic later and helps you be generous when real needs come.

3) Spend with a plan

If you spend everything fast, you'll always feel broke.

A simple plan beats a perfect plan.

4) Don't buy to prove yourself

Buying to impress people is a trap.

It turns money into an image tool.

And it never ends.

5) Be careful with debt

If you're older and using payment plans or borrowing, be wise.

Debt can chain you fast.

If you don't understand it, ask an adult you trust.

What if you don't have much?

Some teens don't have extra money at all.

God sees that.

Contentment is not pretending life is easy.

It's trusting God in the middle of real limits.

And generosity is not about amount. It's about heart.

Jesus praised a poor widow who gave a small amount because it came from trust (Mark 12:41–44).

Quick check (answer in your own words)

1. What does Jesus mean when He says you can't serve two masters?

____

____

____

____

2. What is contentment?

____

____

____

____

3. What is one way comparison affects your spending or desire for stuff?

____

____

____

____

4. What is one generous act you can do this week?

____

____

____

____

Memory verse

"Keep your life free from love of money, and be content with what you have, for he has said, 'I will never leave you nor forsake you.'" - Hebrews 13:5

Action step for the week

Do the "G-S-S" plan for 6 days: **Give, Save, Spend.**

Each day you handle money (even small money), do this:

1. **Give:** pick an amount (even tiny) to set aside for giving.
2. **Save:** set aside a little for future needs.
3. **Spend:** if you spend, spend with purpose, not impulse.

If you don't have money this week, do the same plan with time:

✝ give time to help someone,

✝ save time by planning homework,

✝ spend time wisely on what helps your faith.

Then write one sentence each day:

"Today I showed contentment by ________________________

_____________________________________ **."**

Closing prayer

Father, thank You for providing for me. Forgive me for envy and greedy wanting. Help me be content with what You give. Teach me to be generous like You. Help me use money and stuff as tools, not masters. Amen.

WEEK 47

Love Your Neighbor: Justice, Mercy, and Kindness Without Show

A lot of people talk about "doing good."

Some do it for likes. Some do it to look woke. Some do it to win arguments. Some do it because they truly care.

Jesus calls you to something simple and strong:

Love your neighbor.

That love is not talk only. It shows up in justice, mercy, and kindness—without trying to get credit.

The big idea

Because God loved you first, you can love your neighbor with justice, mercy, and humble kindness, even when it costs you.

Key Bible passages (read these first)

- **Matthew 22:36–40** - love God and love your neighbor.
- **Micah 6:8** - do justice, love kindness, walk humbly with God.
- **Luke 10:25–37** - the Good Samaritan.
- **James 2:14–17** - faith without works is dead.
- **Matthew 6:1–4** - do good without showing off.

What "love your neighbor" means

Your neighbor is not only your best friend.

Your neighbor is anyone God puts near you:

- classmates
- siblings
- teachers
- teammates

- ✝ the kid who gets ignored
- ✝ the kid who annoys you
- ✝ the new kid
- ✝ the poor
- ✝ the outsider

Love is not mainly a feeling.

Love is choosing someone's good.

Three words that help you love well

Micah 6:8 gives three simple ideas that fit together.

1) Justice: treat people fairly

Justice means you don't cheat people.

You don't use power to crush others.

You don't stay quiet when someone is being harmed if you can help.

Teen examples:

- ✝ don't join bullying
- ✝ don't spread rumors
- ✝ don't steal or scam
- ✝ don't treat some people as "less"
- ✝ speak up when a rule is unfair or someone is targeted

Justice starts small and close. It shows up in how you treat the people right in front of you.

2) Mercy: help people who are hurting

Mercy means you move toward pain.

You don't say, "Not my problem," when you can help.

Teen examples:

- ✝ sit with someone alone
- ✝ help someone who is stressed
- ✝ check on a friend who seems down
- ✝ help a classmate catch up
- ✝ bring food to a family in need (through your church)

Mercy doesn't mean you ignore sin. It means you don't enjoy someone's suffering.

3) Kindness: do good with a gentle heart

Kindness is love that shows up in small actions.

Teen examples:

- greet people
- include the left-out kid
- share notes
- say "thank you"
- help without being asked

Kindness is powerful because it's simple.

The Good Samaritan shows what love looks like

In Luke 10, a man is hurt on the road.

Religious people walk past.

A Samaritan, someone from a group many people looked down on, stops and helps.

He spends time, effort, and money.

Jesus' point is clear: Love is not a speech. Love is action.

Also notice: The Samaritan didn't ask, "Does this person deserve help?"

He saw a need and showed mercy.

Loving your neighbor without show

Matthew 6 warns about doing good for attention.

Jesus isn't saying, "Never let anyone see your good works."

He's saying: Don't do good to get praise.

Here are signs you're doing good "for show":

- you only help when people notice
- you post every good deed
- you get angry when you don't get credit
- you help with a bragging spirit

Here's a better goal: Do good because God sees, and because love is right.

A hard part: loving neighbors you don't like

Jesus calls you to love even when it's not easy.

That doesn't mean you must be best friends with everyone.

It means you refuse to treat people with hate.

You can:

✝ keep boundaries,

✝ be wise,

✝ avoid toxic drama, and still show respect and kindness.

Loving your neighbor doesn't mean you accept everything

Love includes truth.

If a friend is heading toward danger, love doesn't stay silent.

You can speak truth with kindness: "I care about you, and this path is not good."

Love isn't soft. Love is faithful.

Real life: where teens can practice this fast

Here are five "neighbor love" moments you'll likely face:

1. **Group chats**

   Don't pile on. Don't mock. Don't spread private stuff.

2. **School hallways**

   Notice who is alone. Smile. Say hi. Include.

3. **Sports / teams**

   Don't trash weaker players. Encourage. Be fair.

4. **Home**

   Your first neighbors are often your family. Be patient. Help.

5. **Church**

   Don't only talk to your friends. Welcome others.

Quick check (answer in your own words)

1. Who is your "neighbor" according to Jesus?

   ____

   ____

   ____

   ____

2. What is justice in teen life? Give one example.

   ____

   ____

   ____

3.   What is mercy? Give one example.

____

____

____

____

4.   How can you do good without doing it for attention?

____

____

____

____

Memory verse

"He has shown you, O mortal, what is good. And what does the Lord require of you? To act justly and to love mercy and to walk humbly with your God." - Micah 6:8

Action step for the week

Do the "One Neighbor" challenge for 6 days.

Each day:

1.   Pick one person you normally ignore.

2.   Do one small act of love:

   o   greet them
   o   include them
   o   help them
   o   encourage them
   o   defend them if they're mocked

3.   Don't post it. Don't hint about it. Just do it.

Then write one sentence:

"Today I loved my neighbor by _______________________________

_______________________________ ."

Closing prayer

God, thank You for loving me when I didn't deserve it. Please change my heart so I love my neighbor. Help me do what is right, show mercy, and be kind without trying to get praise. Make my life look like Jesus. Amen.

WEEK 48
Share Your Faith Naturally: Speak About Jesus Without Fear

A lot of teens feel nervous about sharing their faith.

They don't want to sound pushy. They don't want to get laughed at. They don't know what to say. They fear being labeled "that Christian."

But Jesus calls His people to speak.

Not in a fake way. Not in a loud way. In a real way.

You don't have to win arguments.

You do have to be faithful.

The big idea

Because Jesus saved you and is Lord, you can share your faith with courage and kindness, trusting God to use your words and your life.

Key Bible passages (read these first)

- **Matthew 28:18-20** - Jesus sends His followers to make disciples.
- **Romans 1:16** - the gospel is God's power to save.
- **1 Peter 3:15-16** - be ready to give a reason with gentleness and respect.
- **Colossians 4:5-6** - speak with grace and wisdom.
- **Acts 1:8** - the Spirit gives power to be witnesses.

What it means to "share your faith"

Sharing your faith is simply:

- speaking truth about Jesus,
- living like Jesus is real,
- and inviting people to consider Him.

A witness doesn't make the story true.

A witness tells what they know.

That's you.

You don't need to know everything.

You need to know the gospel and be willing to speak.

Why teens feel fear

Fear often comes from three places:

1) Fear of rejection

You want to be accepted.

That's normal.

But if approval becomes your master, you'll stay quiet about Jesus forever.

2) Fear of not having answers

You think you must be able to answer every question.

You don't.

You can say, "I don't know, but I can find out."

That's honest and strong.

3) Fear of being awkward

Sometimes it will feel awkward.

That's okay.

Love is often awkward at first.

"Natural" does not mean "never speak"

Some people say, "I'll just live my faith, not talk about it."

But the gospel is news. News needs words.

Your life can support your message, but it can't replace it.

People can't trust Jesus if they never hear about Him.

A simple way to share: the 3-line story

You can share your faith in a short, normal way.

Try this:

1. **Before Jesus:** "I used to ______________________________."

2. **Meeting Jesus:** "Then I learned ______________ about Jesus."

3. **Now:** "Now I ______________________ because of Him."

Example:
- ✝ "I used to feel like I had to prove myself."
- ✝ "Then I learned Jesus saved me by grace, not by my performance."
- ✝ "Now I'm still growing, but I have peace and a new direction."

Keep it honest. Don't act perfect.

Another simple way: the one-sentence gospel (Week 28)

You already learned this.

Use it when it fits:

God saves sinners by grace through faith in Jesus, who died for our sins and rose again, so we can be forgiven and live with Him as King.

You don't have to say it like a robot.

Say it in your own words.

How to start faith conversations (without forcing it)

Here are easy conversation starters that don't feel like a trap:
- ✝ "Can I ask what you believe about God?"
- ✝ "Do you ever pray?"
- ✝ "I've been reading something that helped me. Want to hear it?"
- ✝ "Church actually helped me with this. Have you ever gone?"
- ✝ "I'm a Christian, so I see it differently. Want my take?"

Then listen. Don't rush.

Asking questions shows respect.

How to respond when someone disagrees

Use 1 Peter 3:15–16: gentleness and respect.

That means:
- ✝ no mocking,
- ✝ no shouting,
- ✝ no sarcasm,
- ✝ no rude "gotcha" lines.

If someone is angry, stay calm.

You can say: "I respect you. I'm not trying to fight. I just want to be honest about what I believe."

Sometimes the best witness is staying kind under pressure.

When someone asks hard questions

Here are three safe moves:

1. **Answer what you can from Scripture** (simple).
2. **Admit what you don't know** (honest).
3. **Offer to find out** (follow-through).

You can say:

"That's a fair question. I don't know the full answer, but I can look into it."

Then actually do it; ask a pastor or leader, or search in a study Bible.

The role of the Holy Spirit

Acts 1:8 says the Spirit gives power to be witnesses.

That means you're not alone.

Pray before you speak: "Holy Spirit, help me love this person and speak clearly."

Remember: you can't change hearts.

Only God can.

Your job is faithfulness.

Real life: what makes your witness stronger

People notice if your life doesn't match your words.

This doesn't mean you must be perfect.

It means you should be real.

A strong witness looks like:

- honesty when you mess up,
- kindness when others are cruel,
- purity when others treat sin as normal,
- forgiveness when you've been hurt,
- courage to obey God.

A hypocrite hides sin.

A Christian confesses sin and keeps following Jesus.

Quick check (answer in your own words)

1. What is a witness?

____

____

____

____

2. What fear holds you back the most from sharing your faith?

____

____

____

3. Write your own 3-line story about Jesus in your life.

____

____

____

4. Who is one person you can pray for and talk to this month?

____

____

____

Memory verse

"But in your hearts revere Christ as Lord. Always be prepared to give an answer to everyone who asks you to give the reason for the hope that you have. But do this with gentleness and respect," - 1 Peter 3:15

Action step for the week

Do the "Pray and Speak" plan for 7 days.

1. Pick **one person** (friend, cousin, teammate).
2. Pray for them once each day: "God, please help them know Jesus."
3. Do **one** of these steps this week:
    - o   share your 3-line story,
    - o   invite them to youth group/church,
    - o   ask what they believe about God,
    - o   offer to pray for something they're facing.

Then write one sentence:

"This week I took one step to share my faith by ________________

____"

Closing prayer

Lord Jesus, thank You for saving me. Please give me courage to speak about You with kindness and respect. Help me love people, listen well, and share the gospel clearly. Holy Spirit, open doors and soften hearts. Amen.

PART NINE
Stand Firm in a Noisy World

WEEK 49
Answer Big Questions: Why Believe God Exists?

At some point, most teens hear questions like:

- ✝ "How do you know God is real?"
- ✝ "Isn't faith just wishful thinking?"
- ✝ "What if Christianity is just tradition?"

These questions can feel scary. But they don't have to crush your faith.

God never asks you to believe without reasons.

The Bible doesn't treat faith like a blind leap into darkness. It calls you to trust God based on truth.

This week gives you simple, clear reasons to believe God exists—and shows you how to talk about it without acting arrogant.

The big idea

You can believe God exists because the world points to a Creator, your conscience points to a Judge, and Jesus points to God's truth, so you can trust God with confidence.

Key Bible passages (read these first)

- ✝ **Psalm 19:1-4** - creation declares God's glory.
- ✝ **Romans 1:18-20** - people know God's power and nature through creation.
- ✝ **Acts 17:22-31** - Paul explains God to skeptics in Athens.
- ✝ **Hebrews 11:3** - God created the world by His word.
- ✝ **John 14:6** - Jesus is the truth.

Start with honesty: proofs don't force love

You can give strong reasons for God, and some people will still say no. Why?

Because belief is not only a head issue. It's also a heart issue.

Romans 1 says people suppress truth.

That doesn't mean every skeptic is trying to be evil. Many are honest and searching.

But it does mean arguments alone don't save anyone.

Only God can change hearts.

Your job is to speak truth with love and stay steady.

Reason 1: The universe had a beginning (so it had a cause)

Everything that begins to exist has a cause.

The universe began to exist.

So the universe has a cause beyond itself.

That cause must be:

- powerful (because it made everything),
- not limited by space and time (because it created space and time),
- and able to choose (because creation is not a random "must happen" event).

This doesn't prove every detail of Christianity by itself.

But it gives a strong reason to believe there is a Creator.

Acts 17 says God made the world and everything in it.

Reason 2: Design points to a Designer

Psalm 19 says the heavens declare the glory of God.

When you see design, you normally assume a designer.

A phone doesn't appear by accident.

A code doesn't write itself.

The world is filled with ordered systems:

- laws of nature,
- fine-tuned conditions that allow life,
- complex life systems,
- human minds that can reason.

Again, this doesn't answer every question, but it points.

The world looks like it was made on purpose.

Reason 3: Your conscience points to moral truth

Most people, even those who say God doesn't exist, still believe some things are truly right and truly wrong.

For example:

- ✝ abusing a child is wrong,
- ✝ lying to destroy someone is wrong,
- ✝ racism is wrong,
- ✝ kindness is good.

Where do those "oughts" come from?

If humans are only accidents of nature, moral rules become only opinions or group preferences.

But your conscience often speaks like morality is real.

That moral law points to a moral Lawgiver.

This fits the Bible's teaching: humans are made in God's image (Week 14), and God wrote His law on human hearts (Romans 2:15).

Reason 4: Reason itself points beyond matter

Here's a simple thought:

If your thoughts are only chemical reactions with no connection to truth, why trust them?

But you do trust reason.

You trust logic.

You trust that your mind can know real things.

That fits better with the idea that a rational God made a rational world and made humans able to know truth.

Reason 5: Jesus gives the clearest picture of God

Even if someone agrees there is "a God," the next question is: "Who is God?"

Christianity doesn't end with "a Creator exists."

It points to Jesus: His life, His teaching, His death, and His resurrection.

The resurrection matters here.

If Jesus rose from the dead, then God has spoken in history.

This is why Christian belief is not "God in general."

It's faith in the God who revealed Himself in Christ.

"But what about science?"

Science is not the enemy of God.

Science studies how God's world works.

Christianity says the universe is orderly because it was made by a wise Creator.

Many Christians love science. Some are scientists.

Science can explain processes.

Science cannot answer ultimate questions like:

- Why is there something instead of nothing?
- Why do laws of nature exist at all?
- Why should I be moral?
- What is the meaning of life?

So you don't have to choose between faith and science.

You can honor God with your mind and learn about His world.

How to talk about God without being annoying

Here are three simple rules:

1) Be humble

You're not trying to show you're smarter.

You're trying to show truth and love.

2) Ask questions

Instead of only giving speeches, ask:

- "What do you think is the best reason God doesn't exist?"
- "Where do you think moral right and wrong come from?"
- "What would change your mind?"

Then listen.

3) Point to Jesus

Arguments can open a door.

Jesus is the center.

So don't stop at "a Creator exists."

Bring it back to Christ and the gospel.

Quick check (answer in your own words)

1. Name two reasons to believe God exists.

____

____

____

____

2. What does Psalm 19 say creation does?

____

____

____

____

3. Why does conscience matter in this conversation?

____

____

____

____

4. What is one respectful question you can ask a skeptic?

____

____

____

____

Memory verse

*"The heavens declare the glory of God; the skies proclaim
the work of his hands." - Psalm 19:1*

Action step for the week

Do the "3 Reasons" practice for 6 days.

Each day, write one short sentence for each:

1. **Creation:** "The world points to God because _____________."
2. **Conscience:** "Right and wrong point to God because _______."
3. **Christ:** "Jesus matters because _______________________."

Then pick one friend to pray for and ask God for one open door to talk.

If a conversation happens, aim for calm and respectful, not intense.

Closing prayer

God, thank You that You are real and that You have not hidden Yourself. Help me trust You with my whole mind. Give me courage to speak about You with kindness. Help me point people to Jesus. Amen.

WEEK 50
Spot False Teachings:
How to Test Ideas Fast

Not every "Christian" message is Christian.

Some teachings sound kind and spiritual, but they twist the gospel. Some use Bible words but change Bible meaning. Some focus on money, power, or feelings instead of Jesus.

And teens hear ideas everywhere:

✝ TikTok clips

✝ podcasts

✝ influencers

✝ songs

✝ friends

✝ even some churches

So you need a simple way to test what you hear.

God doesn't ask you to swallow every claim. He calls you to be wise.

The big idea

God calls you to test teachings by Scripture, so you can spot lies fast, hold to the true gospel, and follow Jesus with a steady mind.

Key Bible passages (read these first)

✝ **1 John 4:1** - test the spirits; not every message is from God.

✝ **Acts 17:11** - examine Scripture to see if teaching is true.

✝ **Galatians 1:6–9** - a different gospel is not the gospel.

✝ **2 Timothy 4:3–4** - people gather teachers to fit their desires.

✝ **Matthew 7:15–20** - watch for false prophets; look at fruit.

What false teaching is

False teaching is any message that:

- ✝ twists Scripture,
- ✝ changes the gospel,
- ✝ lies about who Jesus is,
- ✝ or leads you away from obeying Christ.

Sometimes it's obvious.

Sometimes it's smooth.

That's why testing matters.

The "FAST" test (easy to remember)

Use this quick tool whenever you hear a spiritual claim.

F - Focus: Who is the center?

Is the message centered on:

- ✝ Jesus and the gospel,
- ✝ or on:
- ✝ the teacher,
- ✝ your feelings,
- ✝ your success,
- ✝ your "inner power,"
- ✝ money,
- ✝ politics,
- ✝ or fear?

A healthy message keeps Jesus central.

A - Authority: What has the final say?

Does the person treat the Bible as God's Word, or do they treat it like a prop?

Watch for phrases like:

- ✝ "God told me something new that's above Scripture."
- ✝ "That verse doesn't apply today."
- ✝ "I know what it says, but..."

If Scripture is pushed aside, danger is close.

S - Story: What is the gospel being told?

Ask: What is their "good news"?

The true gospel says:

- ✝ you are a sinner,
- ✝ Jesus saves by grace through faith,
- ✝ Jesus died and rose,
- ✝ Jesus is Lord,
- ✝ you must repent and believe.

A false gospel usually adds something or replaces something.

Common swaps:

- ✝ "Jesus plus your works"
- ✝ "Jesus plus special knowledge"
- ✝ "Jesus plus giving money"
- ✝ "Jesus plus your political tribe"
- ✝ "Jesus plus feelings"

Galatians 1 says a different gospel is no gospel.

T - Track record: What fruit comes from it?

Jesus says you can know trees by fruit.

Ask:

- ✝ Does this teaching produce humility, repentance, love, holiness, and truth?
- ✝ Or does it produce pride, greed, drama, fear, and obsession with the teacher?

Fruit doesn't mean the person is perfect.

But a pattern matters.

Five common false teaching traps teens face

These show up in modern forms, even if the names change.

1) "God exists to make you successful"

This teaching turns God into a tool.

It says:

- ✝ if you have enough faith, you'll get what you want,
- ✝ and if you don't get it, it's your fault.

The Bible says God is a Father, not a vending machine.

Jesus promised trouble in this world (John 16:33), not a life with no hardship.

2) "Your feelings are your truth"

This sounds freeing, but it's a trap.

Feelings matter, but they don't rule.

God's Word is truth.

If feelings become king, you'll change beliefs every week.

3) "God's grace means sin doesn't matter"

This is fake grace.

Real grace forgives and also changes you.

If a message says you can follow Jesus while staying in ongoing sin with no repentance, that message is lying.

4) "All religions lead to the same God"

This sounds peaceful, but it erases Jesus.

Jesus said He is the way, the truth, and the life (John 14:6).

Christianity is not one path among many.

It's God saving sinners through Christ.

5) "New secret knowledge makes you higher level"

This shows up when people act like:

- they have a special code,
- a special revelation,
- or a special experience that makes them superior.

The gospel is public news, not a secret club.

The quickest way to spot a lie: watch what they do with Jesus

Ask two questions:

1. **Who do they say Jesus is?**

   Fully God and fully man? Savior and Lord?

2. **What do they say Jesus did for salvation?**

   Finished work on the cross and resurrection? Or "Jesus started it, and you finish it"?

If Jesus gets smaller, the message is dangerous.

What to do when you're unsure

You don't have to panic.

Do these steps:

1. **Pause**

   Don't repost. Don't share. Don't build your life on one clip.

2. **Open Scripture**

   Read the passage in context.

3. **Ask a trusted leader**

   Bring the claim to a pastor, youth leader, or mature Christian.

4. **Hold the gospel tight**

   If it clashes with the gospel of grace, reject it.

Quick check (answer in your own words)

1. What does 1 John 4:1 command you to do?

2. What does Galatians 1 warn about?

3. What does the "FAST" test stand for?

4. What is one teaching you've heard that might need testing?

Memory verse

> *"Dear friends, do not believe every spirit, but test the spirits to see whether they are from God, because many false prophets have gone out into the world." - 1 John 4:1*

Action step for the week

Do the "One Teaching Test" this week.

1. Choose one sermon clip, post, or teaching you've heard recently.

2. Run the **FAST** test and write one sentence for each letter:

    o   **F:** The focus was ___________________________.

    o   **A:** Their authority seemed to be _________________.

    o   **S:** Their gospel story sounded like ______________.

    o   **T:** The fruit I see is ______________________.

3. Then read **Galatians 1:6–9** and write:

    "The true gospel is _________________ ." (one sentence)

If you're still unsure, ask a mature believer to walk through it with you.

Closing prayer

God, protect me from lies. Give me love for Your Word and a steady mind. Help me test what I hear and hold tightly to the true gospel of Jesus. Keep my heart humble and my life obedient. Amen.

WEEK 51
Build a Strong Mind:
Faith and Reason Together

Some people say, "Faith means you stop thinking."

Others say, "Reason means you stop believing."

Both are wrong.

God made your mind.

God calls you to love Him with all your heart, soul, and **mind**.

Christian faith is not shutting your brain off.

It's trusting God's Word and using your mind to understand, test, and apply truth.

The big idea

God calls you to use your mind to love Him and follow truth, so you can think clearly, answer questions wisely, and stand firm in your faith.

Key Bible passages (read these first)

- **Mark 12:30** - love God with all your mind.
- **Romans 12:1-2** - be transformed by renewing your mind.
- **2 Corinthians 10:3-5** - take thoughts captive to obey Christ.
- **1 Peter 3:15** - be ready to give a reason with gentleness.
- **Proverbs 2:1-6** - God gives wisdom and knowledge.

What faith is (and isn't)

Faith is trusting Jesus based on truth.

Faith is not:

- pretending you have no questions,
- believing with no reasons,
- ignoring evidence,
- following feelings as your guide.

Faith is not "I don't need proof."

Faith is "God has spoken, and I trust Him."

What reason is (and isn't)

Reason is using your mind to think clearly:

- noticing what's true,
- seeing what follows,
- spotting contradictions,
- and making wise conclusions.

Reason is not:

- pride,
- mocking,
- or acting like humans can know everything.

Reason is a gift, but it is not God.

Faith and reason fit together

Here's the simple idea:

- Reason helps you see what is true.
- Faith rests on what God has said is true.

So Christians use reason to:

- read the Bible carefully,
- test teachings,
- spot lies,
- think about big questions,
- and apply truth to life.

But Christians also know: your mind is not perfect.

Sin affects thinking too.

That's why we need God's Word to correct us.

Three ways to build a strong mind as a teen

1) Learn to think in "truth, then action"

Romans 12 says your mind renews, and then your life changes.

Start practicing this:

- **What is true?** (from Scripture)
- **So what should I do?** (obedience)

Example:

Truth: "God is with me."

Action: "So I will not panic; I will pray and obey."

2) Learn to test ideas, not just absorb them

Your phone trains you to scroll and accept.

A strong mind pauses and tests.

Ask:

- ✝ "Is this claim true?"
- ✝ "What proof is there?"
- ✝ "Does it match Scripture?"
- ✝ "What is this trying to make me love?"
- ✝ "What does this assume about God and people?"

Week 50's FAST test fits here.

3) Learn to control your thoughts, not be controlled by them

2 Corinthians 10 says take thoughts captive to obey Christ.

That means you don't have to believe every thought you have.

Some thoughts are:

- ✝ temptation,
- ✝ fear,
- ✝ lies,
- ✝ pride,
- ✝ shame.

A strong mind learns to say:

"That thought is not true," and replace it with God's truth.

A simple plan for taking thoughts captive

When a thought hits, use the C.A.P. plan.

C - Call it what it is

Is this:

- ✝ fear,
- ✝ lust,
- ✝ pride,
- ✝ envy,
- ✝ bitterness,
- ✝ unbelief,
- ✝ or temptation?

Name it. ____

A - Ask: is it true?

Does this thought match Scripture?

Example:

Thought: "God won't forgive me."

Scripture: 1 John 1:9 says He forgives those who confess.

So the thought is a lie.

P - Put truth in its place

Replace the lie with truth:

"God forgives me because of Jesus."

Then take one obedience step: confess, pray, turn away, forgive, speak truth.

A strong mind is not a proud mind

Some teens start learning and then become harsh.

They turn every conversation into a debate.

That's not Christlike.

1 Peter 3:15 says give reasons with gentleness and respect.

So here's the balance:

- Be confident in truth.
- Be humble in tone.
- Be kind to people.

Winning an argument while losing love is not a win.

What to do with hard questions

Hard questions are normal.

Here's a wise way to handle them:

1. **Admit what you don't know**
2. **Search Scripture**
3. **Ask mature believers**
4. **Hold tight to what is clear**
5. **Keep obeying while you learn**

Many teens wait to obey until every question is answered.

Don't do that.

Obedience strengthens faith.

Real life: building a strong mind in a noisy world

Your mind is being shaped every day.

So choose what shapes it.

- ✝ read Scripture daily (even short)
- ✝ read one good Christian book with a leader's help
- ✝ listen to teaching from your church
- ✝ talk with wise believers, not only peers
- ✝ limit content that feeds temptation and anger

You can't control every message you hear.

But you can control what you keep feeding.

Quick check (answer in your own words)

1. Why does God care about your mind?

____

____

____

____

2. What does it mean to renew your mind?

____

____

____

3. What is the C.A.P. plan for thoughts?

____

____

____

4. What is one thought you need to take captive this week?

____

____

____

____

Memory verse

"Do not conform to the pattern of this world, but be transformed by the renewing of your mind. Then you will be able to test and approve what God's will is—his good, pleasing and perfect will." - Romans 12:2

Action step for the week

Do the "Strong Mind" practice for 6 days.

Each day:

1. Read **Romans 12:1–2**.

2. Write three short lines:
    - **One lie I heard or felt today:** ___________________
    - **One truth from Scripture:** ___________________
    - **One action of obedience:** ___________________

Keep it simple.

Truth. Then action. Repeat.

Closing prayer

God, thank You for giving me a mind. Help me love You with it. Renew my thinking through Your Word. Help me reject lies and hold to truth. Make me humble, wise, and steady in faith. Amen.

PART TEN
Live Ready for What's Next

WEEK 52
Live with Hope:
Death, Resurrection, Judgment, and the New Creation

Most people try not to think about death.

But it shows up anyway:

- ✝ a funeral,
- ✝ a news story,
- ✝ a sickness,
- ✝ a fear at night.

The Bible doesn't tell you to ignore death.

It tells you to face it with hope—because Jesus rose from the dead, and He will return.

This week is about living ready.

Not scared. Ready.

The big idea

Because Jesus will raise the dead and make all things new, you can face death without panic, live with purpose now, and hold hope that lasts.

Key Bible passages (read these first)

- ✝ **1 Corinthians 15:20–26, 50–58** - Jesus' resurrection guarantees ours.
- ✝ **John 11:25–26** - Jesus is the resurrection and the life.
- ✝ **Hebrews 9:27–28** - we die once; Christ will appear again to save His people.
- ✝ **Revelation 21:1–5** - the new creation; no more death.
- ✝ **2 Peter 3:8–14** - Jesus will return; live holy lives.

1) Death is real, but it is not the final word

The Bible is honest: death is an enemy.

It is not "natural and fine."

It is part of what sin brought into the world.

That's why grief hurts.

But because Jesus rose, death has a deadline.

2) What happens when a Christian dies?

Christians disagree on some details, but the core hope is clear:

- Your body dies.
- Your soul is with the Lord.
- One day Jesus will raise your body.
- You will live forever in a renewed world.

Paul says to be away from the body is to be at home with the Lord (2 Corinthians 5:8).

So Christians grieve, but not like people with no hope.

3) The resurrection is not "ghost life"

God's final plan is not floating in clouds forever.

1 Corinthians 15 teaches bodily resurrection.

Jesus' resurrection body is the pattern.

That means the future includes:

- real life,
- real bodies,
- real joy,
- real work,
- and real worship.

God is not throwing away His creation.

He is restoring it.

4) Judgment is real, and it matters

Hebrews 9 says people die once, and after that comes judgment.

That can sound scary.

But it depends on where you stand with Jesus.

If you trust Christ:

- ✝ your sin has been paid for,
- ✝ you are justified,
- ✝ and you are welcomed.

If you reject Christ:

- ✝ you face God with your sin still on you.

Judgment is not God being mean.

It is God making things right.

It means evil will not win forever.

5) The new creation: the world you were made for

Revelation 21 says God will make a new heaven and a new earth.

Then it says something powerful: He will wipe away every tear, and death will be no more.

That means:

- ✝ no more funerals,
- ✝ no more cancer,
- ✝ no more abuse,
- ✝ no more betrayal,
- ✝ no more depression,
- ✝ no more fear,
- ✝ no more sin.

God remembers every wrong.

And He will heal what is broken.

This is not wishful thinking.

This is a promise from the risen King.

6) How to live ready (without being weird)

Living ready doesn't mean guessing dates or panicking.

Jesus told His people to stay awake by being faithful.

Here are four simple ways to live ready.

1) Keep trusting Jesus

The main readiness is not your schedule.

It's your faith.

Stay close to Christ.

Repent quickly when you sin.

2) Live with clean hands

2 Peter 3 says live holy and godly lives.

That means you fight sin seriously because you know you'll meet your King.

3) Love people on purpose

If eternity is real, people matter more than popularity.

So:

- forgive,
- serve,
- share the gospel,
- do good quietly,
- show compassion.

4) Hold life loosely

Hope changes what you cling to.

You can enjoy good gifts without worshiping them.

You can face loss without collapsing.

You can say, "Jesus is better, and He will make all things new."

7) What if you're scared of death?

That fear is common.

Don't pretend it isn't there.

Bring it to Jesus.

In John 11, Jesus says He is the resurrection and the life.

Then He proves it by raising Lazarus.

So your hope is not your bravery.

Your hope is a Person.

You can pray: "Jesus, help me trust You when I'm afraid."

Quick check (answer in your own words)

1. What does the Bible promise about resurrection?

____

____

____

____

2. Why is judgment good news for a broken world?

____

____

____

3. What is the new creation, according to Revelation 21?

____

____

____

4. What is one way you can live ready this week?

____

____

____

Memory verse

"He who was seated on the throne said, "I am making everything new!" Then he said, "Write this down, for these words are trustworthy and true." - Revelation 21:5

Action step for the week

Do the "Hope and Ready" practice for 6 days.

Each day:

1. Read one passage:
   - Day 1: John 11:17–27
   - Day 2: 1 Corinthians 15:20–26
   - Day 3: 1 Corinthians 15:50–58
   - Day 4: Revelation 21:1–5
   - Day 5: 2 Peter 3:8–14
   - Day 6: Psalm 90:12

2. Write two lines:
   - **Because Jesus will make all things new** _____________ (one truth)
   - **Today I will** _________________ (one faithful action)

Examples:
- ✝ "Today I will forgive."
- ✝ "Today I will confess."
- ✝ "Today I will serve."
- ✝ "Today I will share the gospel with one person."

Closing prayer

Lord Jesus, thank You that death is not the end. Thank You that You rose and You will return. Help me live with hope and holiness. Help me love people well and hold this life loosely. Make me ready to meet You with joy. Amen.

CONCLUSION
Keep Going with Jesus

You made it through a full year.

That matters.

Not because you finished a book, but because you gave time to know God, know the gospel, and grow in real faith.

But here's the truth: this is not the finish line. This is a start.

Christianity is not a one-year project. It's a whole-life trust in Jesus.

What you should remember most

1) God has spoken

You don't have to guess what God is like.

You have His Word.

So keep opening your Bible. Keep reading it with care. Keep letting it correct you and comfort you.

When voices get loud, God's Word stays steady.

2) Jesus is the center

The Christian faith is not mainly rules.

It's Jesus:

- ✝ fully God and fully man,
- ✝ crucified for sinners,
- ✝ raised in victory,
- ✝ Lord right now,
- ✝ coming again.

When you mess up, don't run from Him.

Run to Him.

3) The Holy Spirit is your help

You are not left alone.

The Holy Spirit changes hearts, strengthens you against sin, and grows fruit over time.

So don't try to do the Christian life by willpower.

Ask for help. Then obey.

4) You belong to the church

God didn't save you to live alone.

He saved you into a family.

Show up. Be known. Serve. Forgive. Make peace.

A lonely Christian is an easy target for doubt and temptation.

5) Your life matters right now

God cares about your:

- choices,
- words,
- body,
- relationships,
- school and work,
- money,
- and witness.

Real faith shows up on Monday.

6) Hope is real

Death is not the end.

Jesus will raise the dead.

Jesus will judge evil.

Jesus will make all things new.

So you can live brave, clean, and steady.

What to do next (simple plan)

Here are five actions you can take right away.

1. **Pick a gospel to reread**

   Choose Mark or John. Read one chapter a day for a month.

2. **Keep one habit steady**

   Don't try to do ten new things at once.

   Pick one:

   o 10 minutes of Bible reading,

o   a short daily prayer,

o   weekly church attendance,

o   a weekly check-in with a leader.

3. **Choose one fight**

Pick one sin pattern you will take seriously.

Bring it into the light.

o   Ask for help.

o   Set boundaries.

o   Replace with obedience.

4. **Find your people**

o   Get consistent with one local church.

o   Join a youth group or small group.

o   Let someone know your name and your story.

5. **Share Jesus with one person**

o   Pray for one friend for a month.

o   Look for an open door.

o   Speak with kindness and courage.

If you feel behind

Maybe you missed weeks.

Maybe you feel like you didn't grow much.

Don't quit.

Growth is not always loud.

The question is not, "Did I become perfect?"

The question is, "Am I still turning to Jesus?"

If you are, you're on the right path.

A final encouragement

God is faithful.

He saves sinners.

He keeps His people.

He finishes what He starts.

So keep going.

When you're strong, thank Him.

When you're weak, lean on Him.

Jesus is worth your whole life.

Final prayer

Father, thank You for Your Word and for saving me through Jesus. Please keep shaping me by Your Spirit. Help me love truth, hate sin, and love people well. Plant me in a healthy church. Make my life point others to Christ. Keep me faithful until the day I see Jesus face to face. Amen.

Welcome Aboard, Check Out This Limited-Time Free Bonus!

Ahoy, reader! Welcome to the Ahoy Publications family, and thanks for snagging a copy of this book! Since you've chosen to join us on this journey, we'd like to offer you something special.

Check out the link below for a FREE e-book filled with delightful facts about American History.

But that's not all - you'll also have access to our exclusive email list with even more free e-books and insider knowledge. Well, what are ye waiting for? Click the link below to join and set sail toward exciting adventures in American History.

Access your bonus here

https://ahoypublications.com/

Or, Scan the QR code!

www.ingramcontent.com/pod-product-compliance
Lightning Source LLC
Chambersburg PA
CBHW050750150726
48196CB00004B/415